ETHNICITY AND POLITICS
IN SOUTH AFRICA

GERHARD MARÉ was born and grew up in Natal. Educated at the Universities of Natal and the Witwatersrand, he has devoted much of his adult life to social research – starting with the South African Institute of Race Relations in 1973 and including five crucial years as researcher-cum-editor with the Southern African Research Service. Since 1978 the SARS has published the journal *Work in Progress* and produced a series of edited volumes *South African Review* – both of which ~~~~~~ tions as key ven~~~~~~~ **DATE DUE** ~~research material and as ~~~~~~~~~~~~~~~~~~~~~~~~~ ~nalysis and debate in South Africa. ~~~~ 1994 ~~~~~ ~~as himself contributed numerous pieces to both the *Review* and *Work in Progress,* as well as having papers published in the *Canadian Journal of African Studies, Review of African Political Economy, South African Labour Bulletin* and other scholarly journals. Together with Georgina Hamilton, he wrote the book *An Appetite for Power: Buthelezi's Inkatha and South Africa* (Bloomington and Indianapolis: Indiana University Press; and Johannesburg: Ravan Press, 1987).

Since 1989 he has been a lecturer at the Centre for Industrial and Labour Studies and in the Sociology Department at the University of Natal, Durban; he also serves on the Committee of the Natal Workers History Project. Arising out of his work on ethnicity, regional politics and Inkatha, he has been much in demand in the media, interviews with him having appeared, for example, in the *New York Review of Books* and the *Wall Street Journal* in the United States and in the *Guardian,* the *Independent,* and *Africa Confidential* in the UK.

Also by Gerhard Maré (with Georgina Hamilton):

AN APPETITE FOR POWER
BUTHELEZI'S INKATHA AND SOUTH AFRICA

'Admirably structured, superbly documented, and well indexed, much of the value of their study will be to serve as the standard reference on Inkatha.'
— Roger Southall, *African Affairs*

'An excellent book... carefully and thoroughly researched.'
— Kenneth W Grundy,
The African Book Publishing Record

'Maré and Hamilton catalogue in sober fashion the transformation of Inkatha in twelve years from a movement of potential hope for blacks and challenge to the government into an instrument of oppression increasingly in collusion with and backed by the state.'
— Shula Marks, *Journal of Natal and Zulu History*

'It provides a wealth of information on the political economy of Natal and the struggles that have occurred there.'
— Nicolas Cope, *Journal of Southern African Studies*

'Thoroughly researched, wide-ranging, and generally convincingly argued, this book is enormously informative and is destined to become an indispensible *vade mecum* for anyone seeking to understand the genesis and complexities of this most troubling aspect of the current South African crisis... The authors are to be praised for providing students of contemporary South Africna history with a host of timely and valuable insights, and a wealth of important research findings.'
— Peter Colenbrander, *Kleio*

GERHARD MARÉ

Ethnicity and Politics in South Africa

ZED BOOKS

London & New Jersey

Ethnicity and Politics in South Africa was first published by Zed Books
Ltd, 57 Caledonian Road, London N1 9BU and 165 First Avenue,
Atlantic Highlands, New Jersey 07716, USA in 1993.

First published in Southern Africa
by Ravan Press (Pty) Ltd, Johannesburg in 1992
under the title of
Brothers born of Warrior Blood: Politics and Ethnicity in South Africa.

Cover designed by Andrew Corbett
DTP and design by Ravan Press
Printed and bound in the United Kingdom by
Biddles Ltd, Guildford and King's Lynn

A catalogue record for this book is available
from the British Library
US CIP is available from the library of Congress

ISBN 185649 207 9
ISBN 185649 208 7

Contents

This book is dedicated to the memory of Steve Biko (murdered 12 September 1977), Rick Turner (murdered 8 January 1978) and David Webster (murdered 1 May 1989), each one a committed fighter for the South Africa that they believed was possible, beyond apartheid; each one the victim of those who were dedicated to racism and crushing the spirit and ideas of a common humanity.

Preface

The most immediate reason for writing a book on ethnicity at this time in South Africa's history involves the violence that has wracked the country over the past years, and the way in which ethnic identity has influenced this. Many have cast violence in ethnic terms, as if the use of the word itself explains the events referred to.

Commentators frequently label or 'name' events when trying to explain them. 'Faction fights', 'black-on-black violence', 'tribalism', 'ethnicity' and 'ethnic conflict' are often used as explanatory labels, particularly in South Africa. However, as soon as one investigates events and their participants more deeply, the inadequacy of this process of 'naming' as a form of explanation becomes obvious. We have to tell as much of the whole 'story' as possible to understand a particular event or series of events, rather than just giving them a label such as 'ethnic conflict'. We have to reveal relationships, fill in gaps, provide a sense of history and process, and illustrate the circumstances giving rise to such events.

The ethnic phenomenon is complex, and eludes easy capture through an accepted and shared definition. The discussion which follows rejects attempts to relegate ethnicity to the status of apartheid manipulation, bound to die with that system. Equally, it rejects the view that ethnic divisions are irrational or undeserving of attention, and which can be exorcised through calling on 'the people', or 'the nation' or 'the working class' to unite.

Ethnicity can also not be understood as the effect of specific economic relations or systems. It is not a direct result of capitalism, imperialism or colonialism, even though these economic relations may influence the form and path of ethnic consciousness.

Although ethnicity is not simply the result of apartheid, that system carries enormous responsibility for the way in which 'cultural nationalisms' and ethnicity were used for extensive and heartless social manipulation. Millions of individuals – in the name of ethnically-distinct 'peoples' who had to 'develop separately' – were torn from their dwellings, bureaucratically fenced into the bantustans, cast aside when production methods changed or the economy went into decline, and made into surplus people (women, children, the elderly and the unemployed or unemployable).

Apartheid gave us the language of 'homelands', of *bantoe volke*', of 'national states', of Venda defence force, Tswana parliament, and KwaZulu police. It also channelled competition over already unequally allocated resources into ethnic squabbles that mirrored in some distorted way the conflict between nation-states.

The writing of this book also emerges from the specifics of my childhood, spent as an uncritical participant in ethnic group consciousness, acting frequently in terms of an ethnic social identity, experiencing – but not able to reflect on – socialisation into Afrikanerdom and politicised ethnicity. Later, with distance from the group consciousness, I gained a greater awareness of the pervasiveness of such socialisation and the complexity of an ethnic social identity for the individual. But the knowledge of that identity lies imprinted on many of the ways in which I perceive the world, look at other social groups, and am perceived by those social groups.

My analytical interest in the Inkatha movement and the associated mobilisation and manipulation of a Zulu ethnic identity into a political form may have arisen from its parallels with Afrikanerdom. However, with the greater distance allowed in this case, the strength of this group mobilisation and the method through which it was being accomplished was much more obvious to me than had been the case with Afrikaner mobilisation.

Finally, this study was undertaken because of the challenge that ethnicity presents to Marxism, both in its theory and the practice of socialist countries in Eastern Europe and Asia. Few, if any, of the multiple identities we operate with are determined in a direct way by the relations of production dominant within a society. Identities may be shaped or influenced by the relations of capitalism. But the multiplicity of important social identities can never be determined in any simple and direct way by economic relations, as many Marxists argue is the case.

The argument which follows is for discussion. It is not based on any rigid positions. In the same way that the country's economic future is the subject of debate and struggle, so we need to face – and hence debate – the problems of politicised ethnicity. This demands serious research and the development, through open debate, of the concepts necessary to understand ethnicity. Thousands of deaths can be laid at the door of the politicisation of social differences, and such carnage must not be carried into the future.

The primary focus of this work involves the call made on people to respond to an ethnic identity. It is only here and there that it touches on how these calls are received, and how individuals – as members of social groups – accept, modify and compromise these calls in relation to other identities. Individuals are not only Croats, Afrikaners or Zulus, but also women, Catholics, workers, etc. My argument is not an attack on ethnic – or any other – identities, but is meant as a challenge to the politicisation and antagonistic rigidification of any cultural identity.

I hope that this is a contribution to a *debate*, in the manner in which my students and I have engaged in a debate with the stimulating chapters in *South African Keywords* on this topic (Boonzaier and Sharp, 1988). The discussions with colleagues from all over South Africa in the Natal Worker History Project have contributed to my ideas. Special mention must be made of John Wright, Blade Nzimande, Carolyn Hamilton and Ampie Coetzee, another 'dissident Afrikaner', who had much to do with the development of the ideas offered here, although they will disagree with several of them. Thanks also to Glenn Moss for his valued comments and editorial contribution.

Finally, I hope that this work will assist in creating a society in which my sons, Dan and Jo, can one day participate in and be enriched by variety, rather than locked into and excluded by differences – ethnic or other.

Gerhard Maré

Introduction

C an ethnicity explain events and processes, or is it in need of explanation itself? To comprehend why people act in terms of this created social identity, we have to understand what ethnicity is. But we also have to understand the origins of ethnic identities to make sense of how they are used in mobilising groups into action, and to grasp the meaning that is sometimes attached to being a member of an ethnic group.

In what follows, I will attempt to give content to the concept of *ethnicity*; discuss *mobilisation of ethnic sentiments* and *ethnic group formation*; and examine the *implications* of such mobilisation for political and constitutional change in South Africa.

Our understanding of ethnicity is far from adequate. That might sound strange in a country that is only beginning to move beyond a formal policy that rested on ethnic fragmentation for 30 years, and still does.

However, it is precisely apartheid – in its form of 'separate development', 'cultural pluralism' and 'cultural nationalisms' – that closed the door on many serious investigations of ethnicity. Apartheid tainted ethnicity for many local researchers, except when they examined the phenomenon as a tool 'used' to divide 'the people'. The pervasiveness of apartheid as racial discrimination, oppression and ethnic fragmentation made serious examination of ethnicity rare among left-wing intellectuals, in any case warned off by the difficulty of finding a necessary relationship between ethnicity (a set of ideas, amongst others, through which we live our lives) and the economic base of society; between an ideology (a way of making sense of the

1

world) and the central relationships that arise from the way in which goods are produced and distributed.

An ethnic identity is similar to a story, a way of dealing with the present through a sense of identity that is rooted in the past. The novelist and documentor of social and artistic life, John Berger, recently wrote that 'If every event which occurred could be given a name, there would be no need for stories. As things are here, life outstrips our vocabulary. A word is missing so the story has to be told' (1991:77).

Maybe the word that is missing, in this instance, is 'progress', a belief that the future opens up new and exciting possibilities, a better world. Ethnic identities call on what has been, what appears to be known, and what we have some certainty about in an uncertain world. Stories, in this sense, are no trivial matter. Whether they are 'true' is not immediately at issue. What matters is that they are accepted as adequate to make sense of events and behaviour.

However, stories also refer to the manner in which people are called on to make sense of the world, especially the stories that are told about why people belong together, what makes them different from others, and what their collective histories are. This involves those who fabricate, reinforce, redefine and reinvent ethnicities – those who have been called the 'cultural brokers' or 'ethnic entrepreneurs' in society (the 'story tellers').

Ethnicity is not only a common or social identity for people. It is also a term used to explain occurrences. It is the 'name' that has been attached to many recent events and conflicts in both South Africa and Eastern Europe. This short-hand has been used as a descriptive and explanatory term. In this sense events appear to confirm what the users had always suspected or predicted, namely that people are fundamentally grouped ethnically and that this identification explains a range of actions and conflicts.

On the other hand, the term is sometimes used only to be rejected out of hand ('there is no such thing as ethnicity'; or 'ethnicity is all the fault of apartheid and will go away with majority rule'). Any coherent discussion about what is meant by ethnicity – by both its critics and supporters – has been remarkably absent. But this is not because there is agreement on what it means – neither in its every-day usage, nor in the academic world.

'Ethnicity' and 'ethnic conflict' have become part of our day-to-day 'common-sense' language and thought, much like 'tribalism' and 'race' – everybody appears to know what they mean when they use these terms to make sense of the world, and they imagine that all others use them in the same way.

But 'common-sense' usually has little consistency beneath its apparent clarity, with contradictory ideas often being held simultaneously. 'Common-sense' frequently deals with that which we have not properly challenged in the quest to understand our lives or society; often it is simply 'received wisdom', uncritically accepted. 'Common-sense thinking obscures reality', wrote Rick Turner (1972), in his defence of utopian thinking and the need to go beyond what is immediately around us. We cannot afford common-sense thinking about ethnicity. Instead, we have to explore its origins, challenge what is generally accepted, investigate what is valid to people's lives, and present alternatives.

The absence of clarity as to the meaning of ethnicity and 'inter-ethnic conflict' is even more astonishing when we consider that they so readily function as explanatory tools for such large-scale killing and destruction, both in South Africa and in contemporary Eastern Europe.

In a recent example of this, journalist Andrew Roberts set the 'unimaginably war-like' Zulus against the ANC. For Roberts, the unexplained existence of the 'Zulus', with a range of stirring attributes, both explains current political violence and warns against 'a civil war so brutal that blacks of all tribes would look back to apartheid with nostalgia' (*Natal Witness*, 21.01.92).

By contrast, my approach examines ethnicity in relation to the democratisation of society and the opening up of access to information. It will become clear that I distinguish between ethnicity, and the political mobilisation of ethnicity to compete for political power and privilege. That demands that we deal with ethnicity, especially in its politicised form, along with other social issues, including economic transformation.

Building a democratic culture in South Africa involves more than fighting for the election of representatives every few years, or campaigning for the right of political parties to exist. It also requires the combating of secrecy; campaigning for the politics of interaction rather than exclusion; and participation rather than merely receiving decisions and wisdom. It demands a society where questions are asked and answers given, and where the hidden relations of exploitation are challenged.

Democracy also necessitates that the boundaries of ethnic groups should be porous, allowing escape and entry. The tighter the definitions of membership, the more totalitarian an ethnic group becomes. The more centralised the source of that definition, the less democratic such a group is within society as a whole.

Finally, democracy is not advanced by entrenching rights of privileged representation for ethnic, religious or other social identities at government level, or by 'traditional' authority in any form.

Section One

The Terms of the Debate

Chapter One

What is Ethnicity?

If the culture of the nation [in our case of the ethnic group] is only so much wool, then the eyes over which it is pulled must belong to sheep. And so everything disappears, except the possibility of farming (Patrick Wright, 1985:5).

The term 'ethnicity', used to refer to the 'character or quality of an ethnic group' (Mann, (ed), 1983:114), emerged as recently as 1941 (see Sollors, 1986:23). It is one of several English-language usages that have been derived from the Greek *ethnos* ('a people'), and relates to the common character of a group of individuals. So, for example, 'ethnarch' is defined as 'a governor of a people or province' in *The Shorter Oxford English Dictionary*. The same (1944) edition does not contain the word 'ethnicity'.

Understanding *ethnicity*, therefore, involves exploring what is meant by *ethnic group* and the 'character or quality' that such a social group possesses. It also necessitates clarifying the sociological use of the terms 'group' and 'category' to avoid definitional chaos, because that can lead to analytical and strategic confusion.

A *category*, in what follows, refers to the labelling of a number of people or things according to similar characteristics. A category of people is created by an outside observer and the 'members' of the category may have no idea of similarity or even be aware that they have been allocated to a category. We can, for example, refer to income, educational or occupational categories. I might even place all people with green eyes in the same category if I was examining whether eye colour makes certain people more prone to a specific eye disease.

A *group* of people, on the other hand, is aware of and accepts belonging together and being categorised as similar. Members of a group accept their inter-relationship, even though they may not all know other members of the group. Supporters of the same soccer team at a match accept being part of a group, and will frequently act together, even though very few share close bonds of friendship. They are an 'imagined community' (Anderson, 1983), at least while they watch the game.

If we take the example of a *category* of green-eyed people, we might find that people so categorised, if commonly oppressed, discriminated against or treated differently, might become a *group* acting in concert to defend themselves, or improve their lot. They might become 'green eye conscious' in response to eye tests routinely done on them before they gain employment. They might even start creating a history that gives credence to their 'groupness'. While this is an unlikely example, some attempts to give ethnic consciousness to groups are equally far-fetched.

Why do people belong to groups? The most obvious reason is that humanity evolved socially – the isolated individual is so rare that it is newsworthy when such a person is found. From the first bands that came together for purposes of hunting and protection, through the slow evolution of ever-more complex social interaction in which language played a central part, to the multitude of inter-relationships that characterise modern society, humanity has formed groups of various sizes, for different goals and to serve different needs. Families, homesteads, hunting groups, work teams, political parties, religious, feminist and national groups proliferate, sometimes competing for allegiance, sometimes meeting different needs in the same or overlapping membership, sometimes conferring power, and sometimes stripping others of power.

Hogg and Abrams wrote that 'belonging to a group...confers *social identity*, or a shared/collective representation of who one is

7

and how one should behave' (1988:7). They also noted that 'while a society is made up of individuals, it is patterned into relatively distinct groups and categories, and people's views, opinions, and practices are acquired from those groups to which they belong'. Furthermore, individuals with their unique life experiences 'potentially have a *repertoire of many different identities* to draw upon' (1988:19 – my emphasis).

These authors have argued that the process of categorisation referred to above 'simplifies perception' and structures infinite variety. Similarities are stressed within categories or groups, while differences with other categories/groups are emphasised. But this accentuation within the categorisation process is selective, leading to stereotypical views whereby 'the perception or judgement of all members of a social category or group [are seen] as sharing some characteristics which distinguish them from others' (Hogg and Abrams, 1988:20; see also Miles, 1989, on signification). Stereotypical thinking is usually 'rigid and ill-informed', similar to the 'common-sense' I referred to earlier, and requires the same warning against its tendency to obscure reality.

Social comparison is a process that clarifies group boundaries and strengthens social identities, with a

> tendency to maximise intergroup distinctiveness – to differentiate between the groups as much as possible on as many dimensions as possible... especially on those dimensions which reflect favourably upon (the) ingroup (Hogg and Abrams, 1988:23).

One of the most obvious ways of signifying distinctiveness lies in dress and ornamentation – whether this be the colourful dress of many religious sects, the rebellious extremes of punk or the khaki of the Afrikaner Weerstandsbeweging (AWB). However, the 'tendency to maximise' should be treated as just that – a tendency – and we must be aware that groups can and do dissolve.

The distinction that Hogg and Abrams have made between the *social* and the *personal* dimensions of an individual's self-concept is also important, linking to the idea of a 'repertoire of identities' which can be 'called up'. Self-concept is not experienced as an entirety, but as 'relatively discrete *self-images* which are dependent on "context"' (Hogg and Abrams, 1988:24). The particular self-image or identification held depends on time, place and circumstance, and social identity involves both history and social context. The self is therefore both enduring and stable, and at the same time changing as outside factors demand responses. We are frequently surprised by the contradictory, or unexpected, roles that people assume. It is separation through time and context that allow these to 'co-exist'.

The social identification of 'Zuluness', for example, does not determine a constant set of responses from an individual, nor does it include the same set of self-descriptions for each and every member of the Zulu ethnic group. At times, however, this 'Zuluness' can become the dominant identity as its relevance to a range of additional situations is developed. It *may* then serve not only to confer social identity – who one is and how one should behave – during moments of affirmation of a cultural identity, but can be extended to political behaviour and even affiliation in the workplace and other areas where the overlap with ethnic identity seems inappropriate.

The most fundamental reason for social life has always been production for material existence – people have to work in groups in order to survive, whether it be in hunting groups, in agriculture, or in the complex labour processes demanded of assembly lines. However, while many reasons for social groupings relate directly to the way in which society is structured around production (in our case the system of capitalism), there are social units that are only obliquely connected to the economic relationships of society (such as the family). The relationship between a range of social interactions and the need for productive co-operation to ensure survival was easier to see in less complex societies. There was less distance between rites and rituals and ensuring that life continued, between cultural practices and the survival of the group, than there is under capitalism.

In modern society those relationships are often mediated – there is a bigger space that lies outside of production, beyond the

9

clearly defined area of 'work'. There is even a clear spatial distance, in most instances, between work and living quarters, between production and reproduction, and between what is accepted as 'work' and 'home'.

There are additional important reasons for group formation:

- To struggle against structurally determined inequalities in society, the most obvious of which involve trade unions: organised groups with membership, fees, meetings and constitutions, formed to advance the interests of workers in relation to their employers. Revolutionary movements, organised to overthrow what is experienced as oppression or exploitation by an illegitimate regime, also fall into this category.

- Groups may form around the attribution of certain characteristics to perceived physical/biological differences. Sexism, where gender is presented as showing 'different qualities inherent in women and men' and where these 'supposed differences explain and justify the differential and inferior treatment of women', could create the context for group formation (Miles, 1989:88). So could racism where, on the basis of some visible characteristics, a group is 'attributed with additional, negatively evaluated characteristics...' (Miles, 1989:79). The attribution does not automatically lead to group formation, but may do so if a 'race consciousness' develops.

- Groups may form for reasons of social, psychological and spiritual, rather than physical and economic, security. This can be achieved through the 'certainties' of religious faith, or through belonging to a family, a nation or an ethnic group. Patrick Wright has quoted Sartre on 'being French', on shaping and sharing the 'values' of that society, to illustrate this: 'Belonging "is to renew a tacit social contract with all members of that society. At one stroke the vague contingency of our existence vanishes and gives way to the necessity of an existence by right" ' (Wright, 1985:91). The sociologist Emile Durkheim spoke in similar vein of the 'moral reawakening' of the individual in the group, which 'cannot be achieved except by the means of reunions, assemblies and meetings where the individuals, being closely united with one another, reaffirm in common their common sentiments...' (quoted in Moodie, 1980:18).

And in much the same way, Karl Marx stressed the social aspect of existence, beyond the obvious social interactions with nature for purposes of survival:

> *Activity and enjoyment are social both in their content and in their mode of existence; they are social activity and they are social enjoyment... The human significance of nature is only available to social man; for only to social man is nature available as a bond with other men, as the basis of his own existence for others and theirs for him, and as the vital element in human reality... (quoted in McLellan, 1977:90).*

This discussion enables the specification of some of the characteristics of an ethnic group. The most important involve cultural affinity (language, dress, rituals, values and so on); a sense of common historical origin, a unique 'past' (whether it be from common ancestors, a common ruler, from the same territory, etc); and an ethnic identity different from those of other groups (whether these 'others' feel that their identities are important, or even whether they exist or not). An ethnic group can only be a group amongst others who do not belong, and depends for its existence on the existence of other groupings. But while an ethnic group is distinct from other groups, this does not necessarily imply that the relationship to these other groups is automatically antagonistic.

Each of these characteristics of an ethnic group requires elaboration.

Cultural distinctiveness

Small groups can rely on the knowledge of all individual members for their solidarity. That is not the case with large groups – here the community, the sense of those who belong, is 'imagined', in the words of Benedict Anderson (1983). It is not possible to know

11

all other members of what is felt to be a nation. And yet individual members feel a *social* affinity with this community of *personal* strangers. The same holds for ethnicity.

Certain symbols of that community become important and make it visible. They are felt to be obvious, common-sense signs showing that people belong together with those who are in every other way strangers. The symbols for that bond are most commonly cultural: language, religion, the dress associated with cultural history, the festivals, even the values associated with the group – French passion, German precision, Zulu military prowess, etc. Assumptions of sameness are based on these similarities, especially a common language. Physical characteristics may play a part, as in the case of Afrikaners, where skin colour served as a cultural symbol in the mobilisation of ethnicity.

In an article dealing with the notion of ethnicity in the *Godfather* book and films, Thomas Ferraro noted that the

> *rhetoric of solidarity works to organise [in this case the Corleone syndicate] because of its hold over the imaginations and passions of leaders and those in the common ranks alike... (E)thnic symbols function in lieu of formal structures precisely because of their trans-utilitarian, emotional appeal (1989:184).*

No matter its origin, the emotional appeal of ethnicity stresses security and familiarity. People draw together into the ethnic group despite the frequent absence of other expected similarities, and despite other solidarities such as class or gender.

The symbols of community can be added to, invented and reinterpreted over time. Dunbar Moodie wrote, for example, that the notion of 'culture' changed as Afrikaner identity took form – it 'shifted from emphasis on the creative arts to a more technical and ethnic sense that limited "culture" to the civil-religious conception of traditional forms of Afrikaner life' (1980:107). 'Invention of tradition', too, plays an important part, seeking 'to inculcate certain values and norms of behaviour by repetition, which automatically implies continuity with the past' (Hobsbawm and Ranger, 1984:1).

Robert Thornton (1988) wrote that 'culture is the *information* which humans are *not* born with but which they need in order to interact with each other in social life'. It is a changing *resource* for people, but also changes according to the manner in which we think about it (see Raymond Williams (1976), for a discussion of this.) This resource is used (although there is usually not such a self-conscious attitude to culture as this might imply) by people 'to make statements to each other and about themselves. One such statement, perhaps the most significant for our understanding of the concept, is the statement about identity and group member-ship'. Culture creates 'the boundaries of class, ethnicity...race, gender, neighbourhood, generation and territory within which we all live' (Thornton, 1988:26-27). We construct meaning through culture, for example through using symbols to draw the boundaries around the ethnic group.

Thornton has a reminder that is important in analysing ethnicity: an understanding of culture is more than 'a knowledge of differences, but rather an understanding of how and why differences in language, thought, use of materials and behaviour have come about' (1988:25). It demands an historical examination, as do all the aspects of ethnic group formation.

But ethnic groups are not identical to cultural groups. Although cultural organisations can serve to reinforce ethnic identity, they are not sufficient to define ethnicity. We can speak of a workers' culture and a business culture, without in any way implying an ethnic identity. Organisations for the advancement of language rights, or to promote cultural festivals, often play an important part in giving coherence to an ethnic group. Cultural symbols may be legitimated as 'traditional', as that which we have always possessed; cultural events may be perceived to be what we have always done – whether they in fact originated at some distant beginning or are simply believed to have done so. Cultural 'tradition' does not, however, capture the full range of what is drawn from the past to serve the present in ethnic mobilisation. That past, *in itself* and as a catalogue of uniqueness, also serves the ethnic project.

The presence of the past

Ethnicity is characterised by a sense of history and origin that
gives coherence and legitimacy to the present existence of the
group – 'we have always been, therefore we should be now'. This
sense of history is more accurately captured by the term 'the past'
– it is backward looking, seeking continuity for a confirmation of
the present. I will call the specific way in which history is used to
confirm the ethnic group 'the past'. This does not imply that there
is a neutral history that is somehow the truth. The past does,
however, self-consciously serve to both bind, and set the
parameters of, the ethnic group.

Anthony Smith argues that what distinguishes an ethnic from
any other kind of social grouping is the

> *rationale that sustains the sense of group belonging and group*
> *uniqueness, and which links successive generations of its*
> *members. That rationale is to be found in the specific history of*
> *the group, and, above all, in its myths of group origins and*
> *group liberation (1981:65).*

The past cannot be chronologically separated from the present in
this use made of history. It is not simply a set of events in the past,
but is experienced here and now as part of a present identity and
ideology through which every-day life is lived and experienced.

The past, or rather a specific past unique to that ethnic identity,
is needed for several reasons.

* Firstly, it legitimates, through continuity, the ethnic group.
  Inkatha president Mangosuthu Buthelezi said in 1988 that 'we
  have the tremendous advantage of being a product of history
  itself'. Others, by implication, do not enjoy this advantage and
  have to invent their traditions, or live outside of history.
  Through this superficially trite statement Buthelezi also claims
  that there is a 'we group' *because of* that history (BS,
  24.09.88:1). Buthelezi has used history here as the past: his
  claims illustrate the point made by Smith (1981:65) that 'The

more striking and well-known these myths of group formation and group deliverance, the greater the chances for the ethnic group to survive and endure...'

Dunbar Moodie went so far as to describe the Afrikaners' sense of 'their' history as a 'sacred' text. As an example of this, he quoted (1980:11) a review of the *Ossewa Gedenkboek* (ox wagon commemoration book) that appeared in the Cape newspaper *Die Burger* in 1940. The *Gedenkboek* was issued in the light of the 1938 centenary celebration of the Great Trek, used to familiarise hundreds of thousands of Afrikaners with the myth of their origin:

In all reverence, I would call it the New Testament of Afrikanerdom. Again with the greatest reverence I would declare that it deserves a place on the household altar beside the family Bible. For if the Bible shaped the Afrikaner People, then the Gedenkboek reveals that product in its deepest being...

* Secondly, a specific sense of the past serves to draw the boundaries of the ethnic *group* – as a 'template of exclusion and inclusion' (a phrase that I have borrowed from John Wright). Individuals have to accept the dominant version of the past presented in the discourse of mobilisation to be part of the ethnic group. Those who do not share the same history, or even the same version of a similar history, are excluded or exclude themselves. It is also possible to become a traitor to your ethnic past – the past demands loyalty and commitment.

To turn to the Afrikaner ethnic identity again for illustration, Moodie summarises it as follows:

According to their creation story, Afrikaners were Calvinists of Western European origin and a nation in their own right before the arrival of the English.

The subsequent history of this people, as interpreted by the civil religion (the set of symbols legitimating uniqueness and state power), centres on the Great Trek. The latter forms the national epic-formal proof of God's election of the Afrikaner people and His special destiny for them (1980:2-3).

This 'chosen people' notion of Afrikaner ethnic identity raises an interesting issue with regard to the differences between religious social identities and ethnicity. The Christian religion sets out to win 'unbelievers'. On the other hand ethnicity does not usually set out to win converts – 'the past' has defined who belongs and who does not (although it is open to vast reinterpretation and invention). The past excludes, by definition, all those who do not share it. It is not future-oriented with a heaven to win, but is shaped around a past to protect and remain true to. In the case of the Afrikaners, religious events have become part of 'the past', such as the 'battle of Blood River', where God ensured the survival of the *trekboere* against overwhelming odds thanks to a covenant. For a people with such a claim to Christian faith and a destiny, the missionary aspect of Christianity could not be neglected but, at the same time, it could not be allowed to dilute the ethnic group boundaries – especially that of skin colour. The solution was to create separate churches ('daughter' churches) for those who could become Christians but not Afrikaners.

By way of contrast, Judaism marries ethnicity and a non-proselytising religion, although this is not a smooth process. In South Africa, for example, the central role of religion to mould ethnic coherence had to struggle against the faultline of class. More than half of the large-scale immigration of Jews between 1880 and 1914 were Lithuanians aligned either to the labour movement or the political movement for a Jewish state (Chidester, 1992:176). The Jewish 'community' was marked by extremes of poverty and wealth. After the Anglo-Boer war the Jewish Board of Deputies was formed with the specific task of addressing 'the problem of community formation'. However, this middle-class organisation, 'by suppressing elements of its immigrant heritage', could define the 'mainstream Jewish community...as white, English-speaking, middle-class, urban, and upwardly mobile' (Chidester, 1992:178). While there was an alternative labour-oriented, Yiddish-speaking definition of being Jewish, outsiders – through anti-Semitism – forced a common definition on the 'Jewish community'.

• Thirdly, this notion of the past enables action, in that it provides a sense of efficacy and precedent – 'Look at what we have achieved in the past, look at the glory of past moments. Let us repeat them'. It both justifies present action and provides precedents for how it should be undertaken. This sense of the past resonates most powerfully with individuals who need the security and continuity of a yesterday, even if it has been invented.

An extremely conservative use of the past potentially lies in this element of ethnic mobilisation. 'The past' is hankered after, providing a romanticised model for a static present. If the present, into which people are born and socialised, is one in which 'the past' features in a version bordering on nostalgia, then future- or change-oriented events and programmes are threatening in the extreme.

• Fourthly, the past can legitimate existing structures of authority. It can be used to justify selection of specific cultural practices and relationships, giving them the sanctity of tradition, and suppressing others through ignoring them.

The authority bestowed by the past need not rest within a single person. It can lead to domination of men over women, for example. Terence Ranger has found that colonial records often derived what were perceived as traditional gender roles from male informants. Men decided which relationships were 'traditional' and had to be preserved.

Far more recently, migrant workers have called on the past to justify supposedly ethnic characteristics. A Dube hostel dweller, interviewed during the 1991 violence between hostel dwellers and other township residents in the Transvaal, argued that 'We can go to Natal to see our wives. This thing of being away from your wife doesn't kill any man'.

When asked if it was not normal for husbands and wives to live together, another man replied:

No. That is true on the side of the white people. They do have such a feeling but on the part of black Zulu people the husband can be away for five years. They can come back and the wife is still at home looking after the children and there is no quarrel.

17

Another man spoke up: 'This comes from our great-great-grandfathers. They used to come to the mines and left their families in Natal – we are not prepared to change what our forefathers were doing' *(Weekly Mail,* 30.05.91).

In this way, historical processes involving the establishment of the highly repressive and exploitative migrant labour system in the 19th century have become the ethnic 'past' in the last decade of the 20th century.

In a study based on these interviews, Lauren Segal noted that the male migrants perceive the hostels, and their urban life, as partial – 'we are here to work'; 'we know that we are here temporarily because our homes are in Natal' (Segal, 1991:37). The call on the past to justify absence from wives and girlfriends attempted to make sense of a necessity.

Women are not always relegated to an inferior position within ethnic mobilisation, although these exceptions are probably based on class differences within the ethnic group. Afrikaner women were incorporated into the process of ethnic mobilisation during the first half of the 20th century through the allocation of the role of *volksmoeders* (mothers of the nation). This 'role model for Afrikaner women' served as a 'deliberately constructed ideal, the work of male cultural entrepreneurs who deliberately promoted a set of images surrounding women...[centering] mainly on their nurturing and home-making roles'.

But there was an alternative mobilisation amongst younger women who were proletarianised in this period. This involved mobilisation into trade unions that still took account of Afrikaner ethnic symbols and identity, but articulated these within a working-class mobilisation. In the Garment Workers Union, for example, Afrikaner women workers 'linked the struggles of the Voortrekkers with their own struggles in an industrial environment' (Brink, 1990).

A somewhat different focus on the role of middle-class Afrikaner *women* as 'cultural brokers' revealed a more active role for them in a small Karoo town, Cradock, in the fields of language and religion. Butler (1989) argued that these women, operating through the Afrikaanse Christelike Vroue Vereniging, were instrumental in shaping an Afrikaner ethnic identity during the first half of the 20th century that could be distinguished from the political mobilisation of that identity.

A case where an ethnic identity, based on certain traditions, reversed the trend towards male domination was offered by David Webster (1991) in his study of the Thonga in the Maputaland area of Natal. Here males, having to fend within a world of migrant labour, adopted a 'Zulu' ethnic identity in order to benefit from the positive perception that white employers frequently had of the Zulu ethnic group (stereotypical characteristics such as masculinity, strength, militarism and reliability).

Women, on the other hand, had a more favourable status within Thonga society and hence adhered to this ethnic identity. Within this identity 'a woman has a great degree of independence – her mind and political allegiance are her own'; certain kin positions 'confer enhanced status on women'; women play a significant role within 'family councils'; younger women have greater freedom from the 'highly elaborate' rules of respect towards in-laws and 'status superiors'; and women have a right of divorce under certain circumstances in which the husband fails her (Webster, 1991:257-59).

Women are the bearers of the Thonga ethnic identity, and continue to speak Tsonga, for example. As Webster commented:

> *The paradox is that migrancy (and its attendant concept of Zuluness) brings in the money without which no family could survive, but the price is female subordination. In contrast, the Thonga idiom speaks of women's defiance, independence and emancipation (1991:268).*

This is a clear case where ethnic social identities can differ even between brother and sister, reminding us that social identities are held by individuals. In the Thonga case the dominant group awarenesses lie outside ethnic group formation and allow the society to continue, even though the contrasting male and female *ethnic* identities may introduce tensions; as Webster wrote, 'ethnicity is a metaphor for the regional and domestic struggles being contested between men and women' (1991:267).

When the situation has demanded it, groups have been willing to accept an imposed tradition, or invent their own traditions. Hobsbawm and Ranger agree that since the industrial revolution these *invented traditions* have served to 'establish or symbolise social cohesion;' to 'establish or legitimise social institutions, status or relations of authority'; and to 'socialise, inculcate beliefs, value systems and conventions of behaviour' (1984:9). Whether 'true' or 'invented', the past serves similar functions in ethnicity.

For social relations of survival, a sense of 'the past' (even when invented) is most potent in the ways suggested above. It is therefore no surprise that history plays such an important part in any ethnic mobilisation and identity formation. Its potency lies exactly in the apparent 'lawlessness' of modern society where ethnic identities, as *group* identities, give meaning through stressing community, continuity and a point of origin. The further back this is, the more powerful it becomes.

It is in this area that the potentially conservative nature of all ethnic identities lies. A romanticised past may be all that allows some measure of self-worth and dignity in a present that is characterised by loss, poverty, degradation and insecurity. This is the past as refuge; the past as remembered glory.

Groups apart

The third characteristic of ethnicity identified above is that it sets a group apart from other groups. The legitimacy of any group, by definition a part of a larger complex, depends on its uniqueness – in other words, 'we' are not the same as 'them', and are different from the 'other'. 'Our' culture, 'our' language and 'our' unique history set us apart.

For Afrikaners, the uniqueness of the ethnic group was, and for some still is, loaded with sacred significance.

That 'apartness' is not always based on notions of inferiority or superiority. It might simply signify differences singled out for group identity. However, most frequently an ethnic identity is attached to superiority or inferiority, and it is through competition of some sort that the identity is confirmed or established.

The particular status of an ethnic group – be it inferior or superior – may be accepted by the outsiders and may even be reinforced by the outsiders. For example, colonialism was not only a materially exploitative relationship, but also involved ideological domination, shaping the way in which colonised people came to perceive themselves. This cultural imperialism, so well illustrated by Frantz Fanon in Algeria, '…is the outcome of a double process: primarily, economic; subsequently, the internalization – or, better, the epidermalization – of this inferiority' (Fanon, 1970:10).

This approach also formed the basis of the black consciousness movement in South Africa in the 1970s. Its component organisations demanded that the dominated group had to 'restore' its past, in order to give the group an identity and establish pride in the boundaries of the group:

> *The black man…will continue to address his black brother and sister because the events and the rich heritage that are their history have not been made fully available to them in the usual way in which a society informs its membership about the significant aspects of its development. Blacks want to know, and must know, more about who they were and who they are if they are seriously concerned about whom they intend to become (Khoapa, 1973).*

While black consciousness mobilisation reflected a racialised consciousness, and was not strictly an ethnic mobilisation, it was a response to being treated as social inferiors. In a similar fashion the Afrikaner ethnic group has been perceived in a negative way, not only by those they oppressed but also by the majority of white English-speakers. Afrikaners could ignore their relationship to black people because they felt superior to this population. Africans had been largely written out of the ethnic 'other' because people with black skins had been placed beyond cultural comparison with Afrikaners. Black people could not be Afrikaners and, therefore, did not define Afrikanerdom.

The negatively stereotyped image of Afrikaners by English-speakers was more complex in the way in which it affected ethnic group formation. It reflected both a strong antagonism from Afrikaners, a resentment that originated in the British wars of imperialism fought against the *Boere*, and an attraction to the dominant British colonial culture in South Africa. Afrikaners, from a predominantly rural existence, became workers within the mining and industrial concerns of the 'English'. *This* was the 'race problem' early in the 20th century and not the relationship between black and white.

It is difficult to ascertain the extent to which Afrikaner group identity has offered protection against and been reinforced by such epithets as 'hairy back', 'rock spider', 'spark plug' (from NGK – Nederduits Gereformeerde Kerk), etc. Pieter le Roux has argued that

> the historic wrongs [of British action during the Anglo-Boer War and subsequent cultural imperialism] would in my opinion not have been sufficient to keep the fires of resentment burning had English people not repeatedly rekindled the flames by often unconscious revelations of feelings of superiority (1986:196).

Ethnicity, as a social construction, finds potency in its ability to meet the historically specific and particular needs of its adherents. In some cases, adherents include those who manipulate ethnic identities.

But ethnic identities are never unchanging. The boundaries that are drawn around the ethnic group are flexible because the cultural elements and historical interpretations that give content to the group change. Ethnic groups, and those who seek to make ethnic identities, exist within a changing social environment.

There is often a struggle, in the formation of ethnic groups, to shape ethnic identity in a way which suppresses potentially competing identities. This is especially so when identity is being manipulated for the purposes of political mobilisation. The faultline of class poses a potential threat to the apparently homogeneous ethnic group, particularly when ethnicity moves into the political arena. Not all Afrikaners, for example, had the same economic interests or benefited to the same extent from the mobilisation of ethnic power in the 1930s and 1940s.

We can, with some justification, talk of ethnic populism, where a call to a specified 'people' hides a range of conflicting class and gender interests.

Can we now define?

Based on the above discussion, I can now propose a working definition of 'ethnicity', although it bears repeating that the particular mix of elements forming an ethnic identity must be a matter of historical examination, rather than definition. However, ethnicity as an analytical concept is not just a definitional 'invention', useless analytically except to give credibility to an endless variety of manipulations of group identities. On the contrary, ethnicity has sufficient common elements to justify a generalisation, thereby providing a conceptual tool that can be applied in different circumstances. Ethnic groups exist, even if they differ from each other in many respects, are not fixed, and are perceived in a variety of ways by each individual member who at the same time employs an array of other, non-ethnic identities.

The concept of ethnicity, then, refers to social identity formation that rests on

- culturally specific practice and a unique set of symbols and beliefs, the specific combination and strength of which have, however, to be examined in each case;
- a belief in common origin and a common history ('the past') that is broadly agreed upon, and that provides an inheritance of origin, symbols, heroes, events, values, hierarchies, etc;
- a sense of belonging to a group that in some combination (to be examined in each case) confirms social identities of people (members) in their interaction with both insiders and outsiders.

The ideology of ethnicity involves the process by which ethnic subjects are formed, and the way in which they are called on to accept an ethnic identity as adequate to explain

> *what exists... that is who we are, what the world is, what
> nature, society, men and women are like. In this way we acquire
> a sense of identity...; what is good...; what is possible and
> impossible...' (Therborn, 1980:18).*

Ethnicity constitutes the way in which people think of themselves
and others, and the way in which they act upon the world around
them. Ethnicity refers, therefore, to both the call addressed to
ethnic subjects in their mobilisation, and to the outlook and
practices of members of ethnic groups (their social identity).

Patrick Wright, in a book about the way in which the past is
used in contemporary Britain, uses the notion of 'story' to explain
'everyday historical consciousness' which, in today's insecure
existence 'becomes progressively anxious, searching more intently
for answers...'.

> *(E)veryday life is full of stories and... these are concerned with
> being-in-the-world rather than abstractly defined truth... The
> essential thing for a story is that it should be plausible...
> (S)tories play a prominent part in the everyday activity of
> making sense. They help to bring things into the order of our
> world – to thematise events, making them explicable in a way
> which also defines our present relation to them. Making sense is
> a fundamental activity of everyday life and, while it can
> obviously lead to different conclusions in different situations, it
> tends to follow the same basic form. It works, for example, by
> naming things and events, and it accounts for phenomena in
> terms, say, of analogy or causality. It explains happenings in
> terms of the machinations of fate or in terms of voluntary
> intention, and it has always a powerful sense of what is
> probable or possible (Wright, 1985:14-15).*

Both the appeal to ethnic social identities, and the process of their
formation, make use of 'stories' about what constitutes everyday
life. These ethnic stories give certainty, if not in the threatening
present then at least through a clear presentation of the past; they
tell of a brotherhood (and the term is deliberately chosen) of
support and comradeship; they define the enemy (or at the very

24

least the other) that lies beyond the parameters of the group; they mobilise. In short, they make sense of a large part of social life.

The next chapter examines the way in which ethnic identity is formed. To use Patrick Wright's terms, who tells the stories and to whom are they told?

Chapter Two

Born Ethnic?

Ethnicity is a *social* identity, not something that we are born with. However, some anthropologists have argued that it involves an intrinsic identity.

Professor PJ Coertze, for example, wrote that *'Soos elke mier aan 'n miernes behoort en elke by aan 'n bynes, so behoort elke mens aan 'n etnos'* ('In the same way that every ant belongs to an ant nest and every bee to a hive, so every human being belongs to an ethnic group') (1979). According to this argument, nature determines the place of each of us in an ethnic universe of ultimate social security. There is no escape from the genetically determined ethnic identity that we are born with.

Another perspective on ethnic identity focuses not on what ethnic identities involve, but how they are employed to advance certain interests, usually political and economic (see Webster, 1991:245). This approach, which views ethnicity as an instrument, can create the impression that adherents of ethnic identities are simply victims of manipulation to advance specific interests.

While ethnic identities are not necessarily natural 'primordial sentiments' (original identities, there 'at the very beginning'), they are usually presented as having existed from the earliest stage. And while such identities are certainly used in mobilisation to achieve political and economic ends they cannot be explained solely by such manipulation. Analytically, it is more useful to examine the ethnic identities that people are born *into*. People are *made* into members of an ethnic group, as they may achieve other identities. Anthony Giddens stressed this when he wrote that

Ethnic differences are wholly learned, a point which seems self-evident until we remember how often some such groups have been regarded as 'born to rule' or, alternatively, have been seen as 'unintelligent', innately lazy and so forth (Giddens, 1989:244).

The identities people are socialised into usually exist prior to their mobilisation into those identities. Particular perceptions of a group exist before the individual learns and is taught to be an ethnic subject. Determining the characteristics of the ethnic group, and the historical process of ethnic group and social identity formation is, thus, the first task in analysing ethnicity. It is only subsequently that we must examine the manner in which an ethnic group is given organisational form, and whether this ethnic identity advances specific political and economic interests.

These two aspects might not seem separable. The 'cultural brokers', 'ethnic entrepreneurs' and 'organic intellectuals' of particular classes might have a political role in mind from the moment of giving organisational form to an ethnic identity. However, even then we have to ask *why* there is a population *available* for ethnic mobilisation, and why individuals respond to a call to act as *ethnic* subjects in the *political* field? The historical context of ethnic mobilisation is essential to understand why certain elements dominate in giving substance to the group, why such identities wax and wane, whether a specific class project dominates in the politicisation of ethnicity, and why, in other cases, ethnic identities co-exist as cultural pride alongside national identities.

The making and the makers of ethnicity

The socialisation that individuals are subject to in order to reproduce society and to allow each individual to function with the minimum of conflict in daily activity, starts at birth. Babies are frequently dressed in blue or pink to signify their sex, which starts a gender-specific socialisation that continues in a multitude of ways until most people function as gendered beings who have assumed the roles assigned to men and women.

We are socialised into dressing in certain ways, and appreciating certain kinds of food. We are brought up to belong to a particular religion. Most importantly, we are taught to express ourselves in a specific language which not only allows us to communicate and share in recorded material but places us in a specific cultural context – one of the important elements of an ethnic identity. Each of the areas of communication that language opens up – whether it be written or heard, in the form of films, books, education, speeches, newspapers or radio – adds to our cultural and other identities. However, language also closes us off, and sets group boundaries: recently, for example, a preacher was killed on a commuter train because he was conducting his prayers in Zulu; Afrikaans, for many, is the language of oppression, and all those who speak it are seen as having a part in domination. An accent can determine the response of those being spoken to.

The specific language in which we are raised brings us into a historical continuity – 'the past' – that defines boundaries and teaches the differences between us and others. Language serves as the prime socialising means, although it is by no means the only one. But it does more than that: language locks children into a specific set of 'communications' and excludes them from others. In her discussion of French-speaking children in a minority school in Toronto, Canada, Monica Heller noted that

> *Language use is... involved in the formation of ethnic identity in two ways. First, it constrains access to participation in activities and to formation of social relationships. Thus at a basic level language is central to the formation of group boundaries. Second, as children spend more and more time together they share experience, and language is a central means of making sense of that shared experience (1987:199).*

Group history is frequently also the history of a language. The origins of the Afrikaans language, and the date from which it could be called a distinct language (rather than a dialect of Dutch), feature strongly in the formation of the Afrikaner ethnic group and its distinctive history.

Those who led the creation of an Afrikaner ethnic identity were aware of language as a building block. They feared that anglicisation would occur with urbanisation, where English was the language of commerce and expressed the links between the colonial power and the colony. The Afrikaans language, and its use, had to be linked to a larger motivation, that of protecting the *volk*. As Dr DF Malan, who became the first apartheid prime minister, put it,

> *A living powerful language is born from the soil of the People's history (volksgeskiedenis) and lives only in the mouth of the People (volksmond)... Raise the Afrikaans language to a written language, make it the bearer of our culture, our history, our national ideals, and you will raise the People to a feeling of self-respect and to the calling to take a worthier place in the world civilization... A healthy national feeling can only be rooted in ethnic (volks) art and science, ethnic customs and character, ethnic language and ethnic religion and, not least, in ethnic literature (quoted in Moodie, 1980:47).*

Many of the characteristics of ethnicity are presented in Malan's argument. But it is the manner in which these are cast as a *project*, as something that has to be done, that is most notable.

The family is the earliest group within which many aspects of various social identities are absorbed. Thereafter, we are exposed to an ever-increasing circle of structures that can be used to concretise an ethnic identity. These include the educational system (in the case of the Afrikaners, Christian National Education), churches, youth groups, political parties, cultural associations, and members of the ethnic group already in existence who welcome us into its apparently pre-ordained fold.

Religion played an important role in the political mobilisation of an Afrikaner ethnic identity – the church confirmed the *volk*, and justified certain distinct ethnic practices. In the Inkatha movement, by contrast, religion has played no visible role at all, indicating that other aspects (for example, the central role of 'the past' and cultural attributes other than religion) were sufficient for mobilisation. Christianity in this case might have proved extremely divisive of a common 'Zuluness' – a Zuluness whose myth as to the moment of origin pre-dates the introduction of Christianity and hence excludes any presumption of being a people chosen by the Christian God. Making this issue even more complex, the central personality in Zulu ethnic mobilisation, Mangosuthu Buthelezi, is a practising Anglican. This excluded non-Christian forms of religion as central mobilising symbols for Inkatha.

Ethnic socialisation, as with all other socialisations, starts early in life:

> *Young children, like adults, try to construct their ideas and integrate new information in ways that will make the world meaningful and predictable. They frequently reduce the complexity of information by forming global assumptions and thinking in absolute rather than relative terms...*
>
> *In their search for coherence, people often suppress individual variations to support group generalisations (Ramsey, 1987:67-8).*

This process applies not only to the way in which we are socialised into 'our own' ethnic group and accept an ethnic identity. It also involves the way we create and reinforce groups for others, and the manner in which we stereotype those from other 'groups'. Consider, for example, how many people have been forced into an ethnic identity in Transvaal township violence and conflict over the past few years by being defined as 'belonging' to a group (Xhosa, Zulu, Shangaan)? In this sort of case, it is more appropriate to speak of being *categorised* into an ethnic identity than belonging to a particular group.

The full complexity of the transmission of ethnic identity cannot be dealt with here. I have mentioned the major channels of socialisation and communication, where the various structures are co-ordinated so as to reinforce the message – the call – to individuals to define and live their lives as ethnic subjects. But a cultural (or even an ethnic) identity may be shaped by associations smaller than the major societal socialising structures. This could occur, especially, in illiterate societies or where small groups are isolated from others who share ethnic aspects with them.

In much the same way, the major channels of socialisation are not automatically brought together and co-ordinated to reinforce a specific identity. Frequently they meet different needs, and what we gain from belonging and learning from one need not be compatible with all of the others. It is not inevitable that an ethnic identity will be transmitted so that it dominates others, or even that it comes into being at all. Broad cultural distinctiveness is always likely to exist. But this is not the case with ethnicity, as defined above. The emergence of ethnic identity is dependent on the interplay of a range of socialising and other factors.

Ethnicity to serve a purpose

Ethnicity can be an identity that demands no more than a sense of belonging. Or it may have no relevance amongst the many social identities acknowledged. However, it can also involve an identity that serves political and material purposes, or advances these 'non-ethnic' interests.

For example, Afrikaner dissidents studied by Joha Louw-Potgieter (1988) distinguished between their ethnic identity and the specific way in which that identity had been linked to a particular political mobilisation. Most of the dissidents, 'white, politically left-wing Afrikaans speakers', held on to a form of Afrikaner ethnic identity, while strongly rejecting the politicised version of that identity (Afrikaner nationalism). One respondent, asked about situations in which 'he felt more Afrikaans than would normally be the case', said he would rather say when he felt 'less Afrikaans':

> (W)hen I read things that are said by Afrikaners who are blinded by the ideology of apartheid and how they accept things like chosen people ideas, superior race, superiority, using the

> *Bible to justify things... I feel, it's no use, my volk is being destroyed by ignorance.*

Editor of the 'dissident', mainly Afrikaans-language weekly *Vrye Weekblad*, Max du Preez, expressed the separation between ethnic identity and its political mobilisation in the following way:

> *I am not detribalised, and I don't see any reason to be... but at the same time, I see no conflict between being an ethnic Afrikaner, writing Afrikaans, loving Afrikaans, being Afrikaans in my environment – and not a Nat, a racist, or in favour of white leadership (quoted in February, 1991:128).*

These 'dissidents' rejected a politicisation of the ethnic group, or the class-specific ethnic project that allowed some Afrikaners to advance their material interests within the larger South African society.

Dan O'Meara (1983:67-77) set out the way in which the ideological 'call' to Afrikaners to adopt a particular ethnic identity developed in competition with other interpretations of Afrikaner identity. This process showed many of the characteristics already discussed: the nation had to be established as 'the primary social unit from which all individuals draw their identity'. Class divisions had to be papered over, a position clearly stated by Nico Diederichs (who later became minister of finance and state president) in the 1930s:

> *(I)f the worker is drawn away from our nation, we may as well write Ichabod on the door of our temple... He must be drawn into his nation in order to be a genuine man. There must be no division or schism between class and class (quoted in O'Meara, 1983:71).*

The *volk* was presented as being threatened by external forces as a way of strengthening the boundaries of the group: 'our existence as a volk was threatened in various ways by imperialists, Jews, coloureds, natives, Indians, Afrikaner renegades and so on' (HG

Stoker, quoted in O'Meara, 1983:73). Culture, including language, was deliberately used to strengthen a specific definition of what it meant to be an Afrikaner:

> ... *sonder die bestaan van Boerekultuur is daar by die Boerenasie geen sprake van kultuurbewustheid nie; en verder, sonder die bestaan van 'n eiesoortige Boerenasie is sowel die eie kultuur as die bewustheid daarvan natuurlik onbestaanbaar (...without the existence of Boer, or Afrikaner, culture there is no possibility of cultural awareness in the Afrikaner nation; and, without the existence of a unique Afrikaner nation, both an own culture and the awareness of it obviously cannot exist) (Van der Westhuysen, 1950:44).*

It is little wonder that the Great Trek occupied such a central role in Afrikaner ethnic mythology. The departure of the *Boere* from the Cape Colony was presented as a statement against 'racial mixing' and described as the 'most generally self-conscious cultural action' by Afrikaners ever (Van der Westhuysen, 1950:58). Dan O'Meara wrote that

> *Through this strong emphasis on kultuurpolitiek (cultural politics) rather than partypolitiek, the Bond [the Afrikaner Broederbond formed in 1918] was increasingly able to delimit the legitimate parameters of Afrikaner culture, and to direct mass campaigns on cultural issues. This culminated in the Bond-organised celebration of the centenary of the Great Trek (O'Meara, 1983:76).*

The Great Trek celebrations (the *Eeufees* or centenary) of 1938 culminated in a 100 000-strong rally in Pretoria, where the foundation stones of the Voortrekker monument were laid. Unity of Afrikaner ethnic identity (*volkseenheid*) was the message, even if, as O'Meara pointed out, this meant different things to different people. 'By the beginning of 1939, the Bond's persistent emphasis on *kultuurpolitiek* was slowly beginning to politicise the issue of Afrikaner culture', wrote O'Meara. Furthermore, *kultuurpolitiek* was given a 'specific class content, politicising class cleavages in cultural terms' through an onslaught on trade unions and an 'economic movement' which 'made explicit the economic basis and petty-bourgeois character of Afrikaner nationalism' (1983:77). A decade after the *Eeufees*, Afrikaners captured political power.

Terence Ranger (1989) has offered another example of the way in which ethnic mobilisation can serve material or political interests. This involved the manner in which an ethnic identity was manufactured and then accepted to secure specific kinds of employment.

Ranger explored the example of the Manyika of Zimbabwe, and their development of an ethnic identity in response to socio-economic change during the late-19th and the early-20th century. Before 1890 the Manyika shared a common Shona language and cultural traits with other Shona groups. They 'were not conscious of a cultural identity, still less a political one'. Colonial manipulation of territory and, more importantly, the language work of mission stations that privileged a written language based on the Manyika dialect, led to the creation of an ethnic identity around this sub-unit of Shona-speakers. The Manyika migrants, furthermore, benefited from literacy skills that gave them 'access to much desired jobs in domestic service and in hotels' – the 'Manyika' came to be thought of as 'natural' domestic servants in the towns of Southern Rhodesia and South Africa. Even migrants from areas where a Manyika ethnicity was resisted had to capitulate in the urban areas and claim to belong to this ethnic identity in order to gain employment.

Guy and Thabane (1987) have also written about the acceptance of a work-related ethnic identity, in this case by Basotho miners. In this study, they suggested that the 'existence of ethnic solidarity of some kind...has time and again been used by workers as protection in an hostile, violent, and rightless environment'. It is not necessary to explore how the relationship between the technical and dangerous demands of a specialised labour process – shaft sinking – and the ethnic stereotyping of the workers who came to undertake this task, was established. What is relevant here is that the ethnic stereotype was accepted and repeated by the Basotho miners themselves. In the period from World War II until the early 1960s 'management used the sense of ethnic identity and superiority to motivate and organise [the Basotho shaft sinking teams]...while labour used its ethnic reputation as sinkers to obtain better pay and working conditions'.

These examples illustrate the *situational* nature of ethnicity. Ranger (1983:252) notes with approval John Iliffe's comment that 'Europeans believed Africans belonged to tribes; Africans built tribes to belong to' to capture this dimension of ethnic identity formation. The need to assert an ethnic identity at any particular time needs to be explained for it is not always there. An ethnic identity might not even have existed for any number of people during the recent past.

This emphasises the need to examine groups which appear to have an ethnic identity within an historical context, to test their myths of origin, to critically examine 'tradition' and cultural distinctiveness, to probe flux in supposedly rigid boundaries, and to examine the waxing and waning of ethnic identities.

The situational character of ethnicity is borne out by an examination of the particular and changing mix of elements that constitute the essence of any ethnic identity. There is variety between ethnic identities. In one case a myth of origin might be the most important factor that binds members, in another it might be a common religion, and in yet another it might be language.

Even within ethnic groups the stress may shift according to the specific needs of the moment, or the character of the 'other' against which the boundaries of the ethnic group is drawn. In an article on the Central Asian republics of the USSR, Ahmed Rashid of *The Independent* wrote that for 70 years Moscow had 'plundered Central Asia for raw materials'. Against the common enemy of Russian domination, therefore,

Islam is the main prop for ethnic nationalism... but forgotten when confronting their fellow Muslims belonging to another ethnic group, who are potential rivals for better housing, jobs or food supplies (reprinted in Daily News, 15.06.90).

The competition that fragments Islam is stirred up, in addition, by 'corrupt, feudal-minded local party bosses, who are too scared to implement radical reforms and fuel ethnic conflicts to keep themselves in power'. This is similar to the 'national' mobilisation that was possible against colonial powers in Africa. It created a temporary and fragile unity that collapsed in many cases when older patterns of social identity revived in post-colonial competition for resources and power.

Individual members might experience their ethnic identity, within the group and against others, in remarkably different ways – and yet be willing to consider themselves part of the group. Disagreement within the Afrikaner group over whether coloured people in South Africa should be considered as part of the Afrikaner *volk* is an example of this. It reflected basic agreement about the existence of a social unit called the Afrikaner volk, yet involved disagreement about the characteristics for inclusion in and exclusion from this ethnic unit.

Finally, it must be remembered that it is *individuals* who share social identities. Each of these individuals is subjected to a multitude of other experiences that cannot all be incorporated into an ethnic social identity. There is no single social identity for each individual in society. On the contrary, we draw on a wide range of identities. Different identities articulate and interact with each other, so that women, for example, experience and live ethnic social identities differently from men. And at the same time we must not lose sight of the wider structural aspects of society, and the way in which these impact on the various social identities individuals participate in.

Ethnicity and 'modernisation'

One common-sense view of ethnicity suggests it is linked to rural society, pre-dates capitalism and is an anachronism in a modern urbanised and industrialised world. Ethnicity is viewed as a primitive, primordial sentiment out of place in the 'global village'.

In one of his studies on ethnicity, Anthony Smith (1981) has pointed out the failure of both liberal and socialist predictions that rational, urban, industrial, achievement-oriented society, within a world context marked by mass communication, would lead to the demise of ethnicity.

These predictions presumed that the process of modernisation would make ethnic identifications irrelevant; that new forms of solidarity, frequently much smaller or arising out of urban industrial society, would take its place; that the individual, the basic unit of consumption and production, would no longer need support in groups beyond the family; and that where support was needed it would be materially functional (such as in trade unions) or linked to recreational and spiritual needs.

In the USSR it was argued that a new identity within the workers' state would obviate, in the medium- to long-term, the need for the social supports ethnic identities seemed to offer. While constitutional provision was made for predominantly ethnic republics, it was strongly argued that ethnicity would fade away and policy was directed to this aim. 'National in form, socialist in content' was the slogan that informed this approach. Theorists of the communist state had little doubt that its socialist content would make nationalist and ethnic forms redundant in the future, which was expected to be both classless and internationalist (for a discussion see, for example, Connor, 1984).

There was no long-term place for nationalisms or ethnicities within socialist or communist societies. But post-perestroika fragmentation in both the Baltic republics (Lithuania, Latvia, Estonia) and Trans-Caucasia (Armenia, Azerbaijan and Georgia) confirmed that 70 years of socialism had not dimmed the embers of an ethnic, or nationalist, revival (see Suny, 1990).

In Yugoslavia, the Croatian and Slovenian republics voted overwhelmingly in 1991 for independence and a subsequent loose alliance with other Yugoslav republics. This has led to civil war against the Serbian-dominated centre and Serbian minorities within these regions. And in Czechoslovakia the same process of intense ethnic conflict threatens to contribute to the fragmentation of Eastern Europe into numerous mini-states or federal units, with the spectre of long-term violence growing as populations and borders are redrawn.

Do these examples not strengthen the hand of those who suggest that ethnicity is somehow inherent, something near-genetic in human existence? Certainly, many on the far right in South Africa hold the collapse of the USSR as confirmation of the inevitability of ethnic mobilisation and the moral and historical right of 'peoples' to 'govern themselves'.

In the East European cases that I have referred to, as in most other examples of ethnic fragmentation and conflict, one must draw a distinction: there is the spark that gave rise to the revolt and the context that allowed it to flare up; and there is the ethnic form that revolt took. The spark has often been a powerful feeling that a definable group (whether regional or cultural) has been oppressed and exploited by a central authority (the central state in a federation; a conquering nationality or nation-state; or an exclusive political party).

The form revolt has taken has often involved the most immediately accessible mobilisation against these forms of oppression, namely ethnicity and nationalism. Politicised ethnicity (and I will discuss its relationship to nationalism below) answers the need to mobilise geographically and across classes; it legitimates and explains present conditions in terms of a past history of conquest and incorporation (whether actual or reinterpreted); and it provides a multitude of readily-available cultural symbols for group formation and exclusion of the 'other'.

Politicised ethnicity, at least in the examples cited above, appears to be the most appropriate response to the uneven development and cultural oppression which characterised Eastern Europe and the Soviet Union. But, importantly, ethnic mobilisation does not – indeed cannot – take account of exploitative and oppressive relations within the ethnic group itself.

Chapter Three

Ethnicity and other Concepts

The definition of ethnicity as explored above has implications both for the way in which other concepts are used, and for the relationship between ethnicity and the concepts it is often linked to.

However, it must be remembered that the term ethnicity needs to be located and debated not only in relation to specific concepts, but also in relation to the variety of social identities that people operate within. Further study and research is required on the articulation of ethnic, gender, class and racialised identities if workable strategies are to be formulated to realise the goals of non-racialism, non-sexism and democracy.

Ethnicity and class

In studies of social relations in African societies there has been a tendency to undertake what John Saul termed 'crudely polarize(d) ethnic analysis and class analysis' (1979:392). Those who hold to an explanatory framework that rests on class analysis have frequently denied the validity of ethnicity as an explanatory factor for people's actions. Alternatively, ethnicity is relegated to a mere unfolding of class relations or the specific form class takes under certain conditions.

On the other hand, the existence and endurance of ethnicity is frequently advanced to contradict those who argue that class conflict is the major tool for understanding societies. The momentous events in Eastern Europe, in this perspective, have apparently confirmed that ethnic and nationalist sentiments are the enduring motivations for human social action. How, then, do 'Marxist and other progressive writers' approach this 'minefield', as Saul calls the phenomena of tribalism and ethnicity?

Class and ethnicity function on different levels. Class has its *structural* location in the 'hidden' economic relations that centre around production. The existence of classes derives from differentiated control over the means of production – under capitalism a few own the means of production and thereby gain control over both machinery and direct producers. This set of relationships within production creates both the basis for class formation, and determines certain interests which different classes have. But that does not mean that workers will necessarily act as workers, and will definitely not adopt a single worker identity. Classes may exist without class agents (such as workers acting in a way informed by class-specific social identities).

Ethnic groups, on the other hand, do not exist outside of social identity. To refer back to Anderson's (1983) notion of 'the nation' as an 'imagined community', an ethnic group does not exist outside of 'the imagination'. There is no *structured* position in society that determines an individual's membership of an ethnic group, in the way that economic relations determine class membership. An ethnic group may, or may not, exist. The fundamental relationship in society remains, therefore, a class relationship, without claiming an essential course of action associated with membership of a class.

This does not deny the need to contextualise ethnicity within a context of material conditions and class relations. Political or economic mobilisation of ethnic sentiments occurs within a context of class relations and class power. Ethnic mobilisation frequently occurs in situations of uneven development, of colonial exploitation, and of political and economic domination. This factor has to form part of the investigation of the origins of ethnic identity, the re-awakening of ethnic sentiments, and the operation of ethnic manipulators.

However, ethnic identities cannot be reduced to class interests. The relationship between ethnicity and the way in which people organise society around production is tenuous and mediated. Analysis demands that we move between two investigations – of structure and identity, including class identity – to arrive at a fuller and more satisfying picture. Thus, for example, Patrick Wright has argued that

> *while everyone belongs to a class... the lived relationships of everyday life are not in themselves class relationships. The crucial point, then, is that while everyday life is indeed moulded and delimited by social structure, it does not in itself simply express this social structure (1985:7-8; also see Smith, 1981:43).*

At the same time, the powerful mobilising factor of ethnicity is frequently manipulated by politicians operating with a class-specific agenda. This aims to hide the class interests of the 'cultural entrepreneurs'; to paper over horizontal stratifications, such as those of class and gender, through a kind of ethnic populism; and to advance the class interests of the mobilisers.

If the power of ethnicity lies in its ability to mobilise, then the power of class lies in its potential fragmentation or dilution of politicised ethnic identity. Hence, class-specific ethnic mobilisation frequently operates through the explicit denial of class divisions, giving rise to an ethnic populism characterised by calls to the 'Afrikaner people', or the 'Zulu people', in the same way that there are racialised populisms addressing the 'African people'.

I have already referred to the way in which Afrikaner ethnic mobilisers aimed to subsume worker identity and the divisions of class within Afrikaner identity. 'What I do here I do as a worker, but I do it in the service of my nation', wrote Dr Diederichs in 1937 (quoted in Moodie, 1980:169).

However, Afrikaner ethnic mobilisation was not only concerned about the potentially divisive effects of class identities and organisation, but also aimed to win the working class to

41

capitalism – albeit an ethnic variant presented as *volkskapitalisme*. What the Afrikaner 'had therefore to do was not overthrow capitalism but to seize his rightful share of the fruits thereof' (Moodie, 1980:203). As one of the mobilisers into *volkskapitalisme*, Professor EP du Plessis, argued,

> *the new ethnic movement is intended to prevent the further destruction of the Afrikaner People in an effort to adjust to a foreign capitalist system, and intends rather to mobilise the People to conquer this system and to transform it so that it fits our ethnic nature (quoted in Moodie, 1980:204).*

This is very similar to Inkatha's arguments for 'African communalism' as the basis for an economic system.

Politicised ethnicity, nationalism and territory

Neither the acceptance of an ethnic identity nor membership of an ethnic group are automatically or inherently political acts. An ethnic identity is not necessarily a political identity. Members of ethnic groups, meeting all the requirements of ethnicity as set out earlier, may belong to different political persuasions and parties.

But even where ethnicity is not directed at political power, ethnic identities can take on an organised form, and the boundaries that exclude from and include within the group can be clearly drawn. These boundaries may be less militantly claimed and defended than in the case of politicised ethnicity, but they may still be extremely difficult to penetrate.

Ethnic identities, however, are frequently manipulated and mobilised in the service of class and political interests. This is not surprising, as ethnic groups are such strong representations of common identities, and carry such powerful mobilising sentiments within them. That strength arises from the multiple reinforcement (cultural, emotional, historical) that they enjoy, and the multiple needs that they service (social support, historical motivation, ideological clarification, and so on).

The politicisation of ethnicity directs these strong bonds towards a goal that has no *essential* link to ethnicity. Political manipulation moves ethnicity into the arena of competition for power against other groups. Politicised ethnicity (ethnic nationalism) moves social identity to political agency, provides the means for political mobilisation and organisation, and submits the ethnic identity and group to another set of rules – those of competition for power.

Politicised ethnicity is not, however, identical to nationalism. Nationalism can be, and most often is, multi-ethnic – the nation-state, the territorial form most nations exist in or strive for, usually involves a 'plural society' in which distinct ethnic groups 'share the same political and economic order' (Giddens, 1989:244).

Of the 132 independent states existing in 1971, 'only 12 were ethnically homogeneous, representing 9,1% of the total, while another 25 (or 18,9%) had a single ethnic community comprising over 90% of the state's population' (Smith, 1981:9-10). Nationalism is, therefore, seen as the supra-ethnic collectivity – that which binds people together who would otherwise find their greatest sense of belonging in ethnic groups, religious groups, productive units, and so on.

However, while the nation-state gives territoriality to a community of people that usually includes many ethnic groups, it does not exclude political competition between ethnic groups over territory and political independence. This gives rise to what we can call ethnic nationalism. The June 1991 votes in favour of independence by the Croatian and Slovene republics within the Yugoslavian nation-state demonstrated the ongoing power of ethnic nationalism well.

Ethnicity can be boosted by the nationalism of the nation-state: 'Perhaps the single most potent influence on the ethnic revival has been the birth and diffusion of nationalism' (Smith, 1981:18-20). The revival of ethnicity is strongly bound up with the widespread acceptance of nationalist ideologies in the modern world, and with the rise of self-conscious nationalist movements. The principles of self-determination, popular sovereignty and cultural diversity, which nationalism enshrines, lend movements on behalf of ethnic

43

communities a self-confidence and legitimacy that was absent in the case of previous ethnic revivals.

According to Smith, 'Nationalism has also extended the scope and intensity of the current ethnic revival in two other ways'. The first is the idea of 'citizenship', whereby 'nationalism binds together elites and masses in a single ethnic nation with a single legislative will'. This has relevance for the relationship between ethnicity and populism. Secondly, 'nationalism extends the scope of ethnic community from purely cultural and social to economic and political spheres: from predominantly private to public sectors' (Smith, 1981:19). This is the realm of politicised ethnicity.

Territory and space serve ethnic mobilisation and ethnic nationalism in two ways. Firstly, territory can serve as a powerful marker for group identity, even delineating inclusion or exclusion from the specific past that serves that group or its leaders. Secondly, territory may serve to establish the physical boundaries of political claims for ethnic nationalist groups. This can involve the creation of new nation-states in the mould of those that exist around them (ethnic separatist moves, such as those in Quebec, or Kurdish, Welsh or Scottish organisations, or the *volkstaat* demands of some Afrikaner groups; or amalgamation with a larger ethnic identity, such as the demand made by Catholics in Northern Ireland). The two aspects may well function in combination, for example when a mythology of space, of holy territory, of the land on which and for which blood has been spilt, strengthen claims for a physically bounded area. The speeches of Eugene TerreBlanche of the far-right Afrikaner Weerstandsbeweging are replete with examples of this.

Laying claim to symbolic space for purposes of ethnic mobilisation and group boundaries is well-illustrated in the Inkatha case study, which forms the second section of this book.

Ethnicity, community and the people

Both the terms 'community' and 'the people' appear often in South Africa's political rhetoric. While they require careful scrutiny, that task moves beyond the limited aim of this work. However, I will deal with just one example of the use of the term 'community' because it is so frequently used as a synonym for ethnic group. The example involves the 'Indian community', in the sentence 'sociologist Yunus Carrim said there were people within the Indian community who were anxious about their future, but so too were people within all communities within South Africa' (*Natal Witness*, 19.06.91).

The Natal Indian Congress, formed in 1894, has given expression to its members' demand for political participation in the central parliament. Nearly a century later, when the 'Indian community' was offered secondary representation through the tri-cameral system, the NIC and Transvaal Indian Congress were at the forefront of opposition to this form of representation.

The Indian Congresses were, for many years, part of a broader alliance of racially specific Congress organisations. However, the retention of the 'Indian' label while engaged in a struggle for 'non-racialism' came in for strong criticism, and still does, as post-February 1990 they decided to continue with their 'community-based' existences. The criticisms were set out earlier in an article by Singh and Vawda (1988). The authors argued that the history of the NIC showed 'a conceptualisation of the oppressed people as racially segmented', while its presentation of its own history 'expresses the notion of community as being a homogeneous and unified whole...' (1988:5). In this sense, the NIC and TIC's mobilising call to 'the community' is similar to the populist, levelling aspect of ethnic mobilisation.

There is no doubt that the descendants of those who initially arrived as Indian indentured labourers, and were subsequently joined by traders and professionals, have experienced many levels of common oppression and discrimination, even if exploitation was not shared by all. However, 'the past' is not strong enough as a common factor to hold the 'Indian community' together as an ethnic group.

As Fatima Meer has written:

[Indian South Africans'] feeling of common identity was to an

45

> *important extent thrust upon them by their very precarious*
> *position as a minority. Surrounding non-Indians saw them as a*
> *single political and status entity... Yet, despite their integration*
> *into a community, the dependents of the three streams of*
> *immigrants from Bombay, Calcutta and Madras, continue to*
> *maintain, to some considerable extent, the cultural differences*
> *that marked them in India, and are thereby divided into a*
> *number of sub-groups, most conspicuously recognisable by*
> *language and religion (1969:60-61).*

'Community', whether used in this wide sense to refer to 'Indian' people in South Africa, or to smaller residential or geographic units, should not be taken for granted as a common-sense expression of group belonging. As with ethnicity, questions should be asked about the situational relevance of the term for participants or members, and the specific content given to it.

On the other hand, the appeal to community may well serve to provide a cohesion that cuts across ethnic divisions – this has been the case with some residentially-constituted appeals to 'community'. The ideological notion of 'the people', while similarly problematic as an analytical category, may well serve to bond rather than fragment.

Ethnicity and gender

Gender refers to the roles attributed to men and women through socialisation, and the relationships that exist between them. When we examine the gender aspect of ethnic group formation it is, therefore, necessary to question the characteristics attributed to both male and female ethnic subjects, whether it be the 'warrior' or the 'mother of the nation'.

Ethnic mobilisation is never gender neutral. The constitution of ethnic social identities occurs within the general social relations of society. Hierarchical relationships often accompany 'tradition' and the 'traditional' roles that are ascribed to men and women within the ethnic project.

The gender dimension of ethnicity is both under-researched and under-theorised. It is further complicated by male presentation of ethnic homogeneity, and a presumption that the roles ascribed to males and females within the ethnic group are accepted and unproblematic. The case of the Tsonga, described in chapter two, illustrates that this presentation should not be accepted at face value.

The gender dimension of ethnic group formation needs to be historically situated. As Walker notes:

> *it should... be clear that a static and culture-bound understanding of gender is inadequate... The meaning of 'woman' was not the same in precolonial as it was in twentieth century southern Africa... The differences went beyond obvious ones in the type of work and responsibilities assigned to women, to encompass the structural significance of the sexual division of labour within these societies, as well as the social meaning assigned to women's roles (Walker, 1990:26).*

That meaning is assigned not only by the participants (male and female) in the ethnic social identity, but also by those who stand outside of it. The term 'ethnic', and the use of what is deemed to be ethnic, is mobilised in fashion, food and tourism, to name but a few areas; in many cases it reflects what outsiders want to sell rather than an accepted version by those who are part of the ethnic group. Women feature prominently in this 'ethnic sales drive'.

The family is a strong element in ethnic mobilisation, serving to reinforce not only authority of age and parents but also of the gender hierarchy that exists in the family. The ideal of the family provides a notion of continuity, stability and order. For example, within Afrikaner ethnic mobilisation, the family as a patriarchal, conservative and religious social unit was stressed as an element binding the ethnic group:

> *In ons volkswording het die huisgesin so 'n sentrale plek ingeneem en in die bepaling van die kultuur van ons nasie was dit sodanig van deurslaggewende betekenis dat die Afrikanerdom met reg as 'n by uitstek 'familiale' volk bestempel*

kan word (In the formation of our ethnic group the family played such a central role and in the determination of the culture of our nation it was of such cardinal importance that the Afrikaner nation can justifiably be called an essentially 'familial' ethnic group (Cronjé, 1945:309).

Ethnicity, tribalism and race

It is common, at least in an African context, to refer to ethnic identities as 'tribal'. So, for example, the term 'tribe' is often used in reference to Afrikaner identity – as in 'the white tribe of Africa', for example. There is some suggestion that this is appropriate only in Africa. Certainly, neither Serbs nor Croatians are ever referred to as tribes. Neither are the Quebecois in Canada.

Collapsing ethnic identities into tribalism is clearly incorrect: a 'tribal' or clan unit or chiefdom refers to a much smaller functional societal grouping under pre-capitalist conditions, drawing a number of smaller homestead productive units together. A sense of cultural and historical group belonging, equated with ethnicity, was absent.

Turning to race, the authors Phizacklea and Miles wrote that

Viewed historically, the 'race' concept has tended to be used when people are being classified in terms of their physical characteristics: thus, if a population consists of two groups which are clearly physically distinguishable, and significance is attached to some aspect of this distinguishability, it is usually concluded that the two groups belong to different 'races' (1980:21).

Despite most South African political organisations' commitment to a non-racial future, a common-sense belief in the existence of 'races' permeates every facet of our society. It needs little to break through the slogans and expose the manner in which the laudable commitment has little content and no programme. Most people believe that 'races' exist, in the weakest sense of a categorisation of physical differences. Many, if not most, also accept that these physical differences are linked to cultural attributes, patterns of behaviour, ability, and so on.

Robert Miles (1989) has argued that a discourse of 'race', having lost all serious validity in the biological sciences where genetics has displaced it, rests on a process of signification. This refers to 'the representational process by which meanings are attributed to particular objects, features and processes'. To arrive at a notion of 'race' two selections are made in the process of signification: the first selects physical features 'as a means of classification and categorisation' of people; the second selection is from the range of 'somatic characteristics' which signify 'a supposed difference between human beings' (1989:70-71). These 'races' are then frequently deemed to have distinct cultural characteristics – really a third level of selection and signification.

When 'social relations between people have been structured by the signification of human biological characteristics in such a way as to define and construct differentiated social collectivities', a process of *racialisation* has occurred. These relations vary historically (Miles, 1989:75). *Racism* then refers to a process of racialisation where 'the group so identified must be attributed with additional, negatively evaluated characteristics and/or must be represented as inducing negative consequences for any other' (Miles, 1989:79).

Using Miles' argument, we can see quite clearly how racialisation occurred in South Africa, leading to policies based essentially on the supposed existence of 'races', where the practices of racism permeated much of social and inter-personal relations. The ideological and organisational practices of resistance tended to operate within the same terrain of racialised social and political interaction, with the Congress Alliance of the 1950s involving a 'multi-racial' alliance of four 'racial' organisations. In this regard, it is interesting to note that Robert Sobukwe of the splinter Pan-Africanist Congress argued that 'multi-racialism' perpetuated divisions and that 'there is but one race, the human race' (see Lodge, 1983:85).

Racialisation occurs on the basis of the signification of

physical characteristics. This is very different from the basis of ethnicity. As diverse ethnic groups can exist within nations, so ethnic groups can exist within the racialised collectivity. It is probable that all members of an ethnic group will belong to a single racialised social unit, but this is not of the essence. While all members of the 'Zulu nation' are black, for example, the Afrikaner ethnic group has come under assault through its need to define the position of 'coloured' people who in all essential aspects qualify for inclusion.

Section Two

Zulu Nation

Chapter Four

'Brothers Born of Warrior Stock'

In this second section I examine the specific example of ethnic mobilisation into the 'Zulu nation'. This is an important case. Understanding it may assist in shaping a South Africa where divisions are seen as resolvable, rather than as fixed, inherent and trans-historical. In addition, the case of Zulu ethnic mobilisation illustrates many of the more theoretical points made in section one.

The focus of this discussion is on South Africa. But ethnicity is not a local or African phenomenon, akin to or synonymous with 'tribalism'. Nor does the selection of a Zulu ethnic social identity as an example deny that other ethnic mobilisations are occurring.

Ethnic groups, and political mobilisation of ethnic sentiments, occur in most parts of the world. However, to understand each case, we have to examine its particular unfolding and specific 'mix' of elements, using the general tools suggested in the first section of this discussion. We have to explore the reasons why ethnic sentiments find fertile ground in some cases, but not in others; and we have to see who the prime mobilisers are, and what interests the mobilisation serves.

There are many similarities and comparisons to be drawn between specific cases of ethnic group formation and ethnic conflict. This section deals with the three elements of the definition of ethnicity developed from these similarities in the previous section – cultural particularity; historical origin; and group boundaries. It is, however, not possible to separate these three elements neatly: they exist in their interaction, thereby composing an ethnic identity and an ethnic group.

A study of the Inkatha movement adds to our understanding of ethnic mobilisation in a number of ways. It provides a clear example of the use of a claimed cultural distinctiveness; it illustrates how historical legitimacy for the ethnic group is presented in mobilisation; it shows how the group is pitched against other groups; it illustrates the politicisation of ethnicity mobilised within an exclusive organisation; and, finally, it highlights the centrality of a single symbol – the person of Chief Mangosuthu Buthelezi – a factor not present in all instances of ethnic mobilisation.

The example of Inkatha is discussed to illustrate ethnic group formation. Not all varieties of 'Zulu' ethnic identity are encapsulated in this movement (now called the Inkatha Freedom Party – IFP). However, the Inkatha case has been the most consistent, most self-conscious and best publicised version of ethnic mobilisation in South Africa, along with Afrikaner mobilisation in the first half of the 20th century. This leaves opponents of Inkatha under a distinct disadvantage if they wish to salvage any 'Zulu' ethnic social identity separate from the IFP.

This section concentrates on the process of ethnic group formation and definition, and not on the political history of the Inkatha movement (see Maré and Hamilton, 1987; and Mzala, 1988:116-133, for such a history). However, a brief overview is necessary to periodise stages in that process.

Thereafter, the mobilising strategies, symbols, agents, structures and practices employed by Buthelezi and Inkatha are discussed. Many of these coincide or overlap with, or were made available by, apartheid policy (the educational system in KwaZulu used with such vigour by Inkatha in its mobilising strategy, for example).

Inkatha: a brief history

Apartheid's legacy exists as much in the political role it has attached to ethnicity and cultural diversity as in poverty, population relocation, death and illiteracy. 'Homeland independence' can be undone through legislation because it was largely created through legislation; the services provided through the bantustan departments can become part of national state structures or democratic regional government; development projects can be undertaken to start a process of redistribution of resources and opportunities. However, the depth of ethnic identification and its manipulation for political ends will be less easy to wipe away. Political manipulation of ethnicity has permeated the very transmission of ideas; ethnicity has informed the actions of South Africans over many years because it seemed to make sense of the every-day world.

That 'sense', for example, led to frequent clashes over scarce resources being expressed in ethnic terms. Clashes over land, in particular, were understood in ethnic terms, because that was the basis on which land allocation under apartheid was made, and the way in which borders were drawn between people.

From its formation in 1975, leaders of Inkatha relied heavily on the power of chiefs in rural areas, even though these chiefs had to be convinced that the new movement was not going to peripheralise them or dilute their powers.

Twenty years earlier, the young Gatsha Buthelezi contentiously came to lead the Buthelezi clan as chief, with government approval. When Buthelezi decided to fight for this chieftaincy, he admitted that an alternative political path had been available to him. This would have led through the African National Congress Youth League, of which he had briefly been a member, to a legal career and articles with then-Communist Party member and lawyer Rowley Arenstein, and continuation in the mainstream of African nationalist politics. Buthelezi did not abandon either Arenstein or the political symbolism of the ANC, but the contradictions that have driven Inkatha into an increasingly conservative camp were etched into his personal and organisational history at that time.

Having to atone for his role as a troublesome student (in the eyes of the University of Fort Hare authorities) and member of the ANC Youth League – both of them blots in the copybook of chieftainship – Buthelezi served a period in the Department of Native Affairs. He became acting chief in 1953. Two years before this, the Bantu Authorities Act had confirmed the exclusion of Africans from central authority, and reaffirmed that they would be subject to a system of indirect rule. In 1957 the National Party government formally installed him as head of the Buthelezi 'tribe'. Buthelezi thereby became an agent of administration and an element of 'the past' he was both part of and attempting to recreate.

With the choice that Buthelezi made in the 1950s, his own political career started its parallel, and at times criss-crossing, path with the course the state had charted for African politics. Both the National Party and Buthelezi – and later Inkatha – drew on the sediment of the past to help shape the present.

In 1959, the year in which the ethnic fragmentation of the apartheid policy was given legislative form in the Promotion of Bantu Self-Government Act, Minister of Bantu Administration and Development De Wet Nel, expressed this relationship between the past and the present in the following way:

> The Zulu is proud to be a Zulu and the Xhosa proud to be a Xhosa and the Venda is proud to be a Venda, just as proud as they were a hundred years ago. The lesson we have learnt from history during the past three hundred years is that these ethnic groups, the whites as well as the Bantu, sought their greatest fulfillment, their greatest happiness and the best mutual relations on the basis of separate and individual development... the only basis on which peace, happiness and mutual confidence could be built up (quoted in Moodie, 1980:266).

However, it was not only *ideas* of the past that lived on in this way. The remnants of the past were mobilised to serve the aspirations of the present. They were mediated through and given form in an ethnic identity, which was then employed for political mobilisation, control and direction. Through this, the National Party gave organisational and spatial form to the racial domination of whites. It developed the paternalistic 'guardianism' of the pre-1948 segregation period into apartheid. The blatant racism of this policy was sugared with the idea of 'cultural nationalisms' and eventual 'independence' for the bantustan areas, modelled on what the Afrikaners said they had wanted for themselves – an ethnic pride, their own 'homeland' and political identity. These were presented in the language of decolonisation that was sweeping Africa during the 1950s. It was this policy and its effects that placed ethnic mobilisation firmly on the agenda for African 'ethnic entrepreneurs' or 'brokers'.

In Natal, chiefs, the Zulu royal house, and the symbol of the 'Zulu nation' were mobilised not only by successive colonial, Union and apartheid administrations, but also by both progressive and reactionary African interests. This is what Buthelezi became part of in the 1950s: a broadly agreed-upon Zulu identity, acknowledged by both 'members' ('Zulus', as defined by different and competing interests), and outsiders (the apartheid state which had to find a basis of legitimation for its policies).

However, in the 1950s, this Zulu identity existed in a much looser form: it mingled with an ANC-led national identity (with Chief Albert Luthuli symbolising this as both a Zulu chief and the last president of the ANC before it was banned in 1960).

During the 1960s, Buthelezi apparently agonised over whether to take part in the new role envisaged for the tribal authorities which he had become part of in the 1950s. When it was made clear, according to Buthelezi, that there was no choice, he allowed the constituent tribal authorities to elect him to lead the regional authority within which his tribal authority fell. (It is not clear why the widespread resistance of chiefs to this new role, which Buthelezi claimed existed at the time, could not have been translated into a boycott). Then, in 1970, he came to head the pinnacle of the Promotion of Bantu Self-Government Act pyramid for the Zulus, the Zululand Territorial Authority, being unanimously elected by the regional authorities then in existence.

Initially, Buthelezi advanced two justifications for participation in these undemocratic, apartheid-created, institutions: on the one hand, he presented the decision as a selfless *choice* to prevent a stooge from being appointed in his place; on the other hand, he claimed he was *destined* to lead a Zulu nation that pre-existed apartheid and colonialism, covering a territory, a 'kingdom' and a state that dated back to the 1820s and 1830s. Over time, as Buthelezi consolidated his political defeat of the Zulu king, Goodwill Zwelethini, the latter justification came to dominate, with additional claims being made for the strategy of 'working within the system and changing it from within'.

Buthelezi refused to follow the politically-suicidal route of 'independence' for the KwaZulu 'homeland'. In 1972 the Zululand Territorial Authority became the KwaZulu Legislative Assembly. In 1975 Inkatha was formed as an exclusively Zulu movement. In 1977 KwaZulu entered the next stage in self-government, with its powers now exceeding those of the second-tier provincial government, and based from 1984 in multi-million Rand legislative assembly buildings in the new capital, Ulundi. These were paid for through a re-allocation within its own meagre budget, which had to cover education, pensions, social security, etc. In 1977 Inkatha changed its constitution to welcome all other African people into membership – albeit with little success on the ground.

For Buthelezi, politics in KwaZulu during the first eight years of the 1970s was dominated by two struggles. The first involved a battle against state attempts to create an alternative Zulu tradition through some chiefs and disgruntled traders, using the king as a central symbolic figure. Within this scheme, the state envisaged an executive role for the king, and the removal of Buthelezi, who government viewed as impertinent in his rejection of 'independence' for KwaZulu. Buthelezi's second, and not totally separate struggle, was against opponents of his close links with state development agencies, and his co-operation with big capital. These opponents – a section of the Zulu trading class – felt threatened by the economic impact of the alliance with big capital, and were disgruntled by the mode of operation of the Bantu Investment Corporation (forerunner to the KwaZulu Development Corporation).

The hand of Buthelezi and Inkatha was strengthened during this period through African National Congress support for their

57

political agenda. One powerful set of political symbols of mobilisation arose out of the identification of Inkatha with a revived ANC. Inkatha colours, its political myth of origin and some leadership figures were drawn from aspects of ANC tradition, especially its conservative branch in Natal prior to its banning. Another set of symbols were drawn from Zulu ethnicity.

There is a fundamental way, though, in which these two sets of symbols and traditions are entangled. Buthelezi makes much of the 'Zulu' character of many personalities in the ANC before 1960, and decries the 'dilution' of the Zulu and African presence through the subsequent non-racial policy of the ANC. Thus, for example, in his study of the Inkatha 'civics' syllabus for schools, Mdluli (1987) found that

> the selection of leaders (from the ANC)... throws further light onto the slant of Ubuntu-botho. All the leaders who are selected are either Zulu-speaking Natalians or have strong connections with the Zulu royal family... What is of particular significance about these leaders... is the connection drawn between what they did or stood for and the actions of Inkatha and/or the KwaZulu government.

Mdluli found that 'there is a huge gap (in the Inkatha version of resistance history) between the 1960s and 1975', while the current ANC leadership is practically ignored (only Mandela, Tambo and Sisulu are referred to on occasion).

Inkatha's leaders presented their organisation as a continuation of the ANC after a 15-year lull: 'Inkatha was founded in response to the political vacuum that had been created when the African National Congress and Pan-Africanist Congress were banned', and it was formed 'on the principles of the founding fathers of the ANC', said Inkatha secretary general Oscar Dhlomo (Swart interview with Oscar Dhlomo, 1984).

In one way, it is quite accurate to refer to a 'Zulu' presence in the ANC: there were many Zulu-speaking leaders in the organisation who came from this part of South Africa, but it is also true that they frequently showed a degree of Zulu chauvinism and

a tendency to form regional factions. Beall et al (1986:22)
commented that while Dube had been the first president of the
ANC, formed to co-ordinate *national* resistance to political
exclusion and territorial confinement of Africans, he was replaced
in 1917 and from

> *that date... until his death in 1946 he created a regional base*
> *that stood in conflict with the national African National*
> *Congress. His Natal Native Congress left a legacy of tension*
> *that was only resolved with the election of chief Albert Luthuli*
> *as president of the regional (1951) and then of the national*
> *Congress (1952).*

Buthelezi has ignored these difficulties with the ANC tradition he
presents.

The political role of Albert Luthuli, president of the ANC at the
time of its banning and a Zulu chief stripped of this function by
the NP government, is an essential link in the tradition created and
presented by Inkatha. Buthelezi frequently claims links with Chief
Luthuli, with his family and with his memory. Inkatha even claims
that in 'a symbolic meeting between Chief Luthuli and the Hon.
Chief MG Buthelezi in the 1960s, the heritage of the leadership of
the liberation struggle was passed on to the Hon. Chief Buthelezi'
(Inkatha, 1983:12).

Buthelezi pulled these various traditions together in a speech
made at the unveiling of the tombstone of H Selby Msimang and
his wife. He first established his own position in relation to
Msimang ('founder member of the banned African National
Congress'), and then linked the ANC of Msimang and Inkatha:

> *He was a link together with Mr Champion between the old*
> *founding fathers of the African National Congress and the*
> *leadership of Inkatha. Mr. Msimang's membership of Inkatha*
> *justified what I say so often – that Inkatha is structured on the*
> *ideals of the banned African National Congress as propounded*
> *in 1912 by the founding fathers. He was one of those founding*
> *fathers whose membership of Inkatha testified to the fact that it*

was not us in Inkatha who have deviated from those ideals. The
ideals of the founding fathers who were descendants of black
warriors were structured on the foundation of non-violence and
negotiations... He saw us as forming a continuum of those very
ideals... We will not be influenced away from those ideals by
any elitist clique whatever they call themselves (BS, 06.04.87).

At the end of the 1970s, Inkatha and Buthelezi's balancing act
between a regional and Zulu mobilisation, and an African
nationalist mobilisation, changed. This occurred through a rupture
of the relationship with the ANC, and with the defeat of attempts
to create an alternative political position under the leadership of
the Zulu king. The 1980s saw a new direction from Inkatha,
independent from any major concern with national politics and
national political symbols. Inkatha had defined itself outside of the
mainstream of political struggle. That current was defined by 'the
youth'; by the ANC with its strategies of armed struggle, sanctions
and ungovernability; by the United Democratic Front (UDF,
formed in 1983) and the Congress of South African Trade Unions
(Cosatu, launched in 1985); and by the organisationally-loose
formation that became known as the 'mass democratic movement'.

For Inkatha, the 1980s can be summarised as a period of
regional consolidation. It was characterised by blatant and
dangerous ethnic political mobilisation; structural integration of
the KwaZulu bantustan and Natal Provincial Administration;
drafting of blueprints for regional reform through the Buthelezi
Commission and the Indaba; formation of alliances with
conservative political and moneyed interests; and defining 'the
enemy' in ever-clearer terms.

The enemy, for Inkatha, involved not only political opponents
but included 'Zulus' who rejected the version of politicised
ethnicity propounded by the Inkatha leadership and the Zulu king.
Castigating and threatening these 'traitors' to the Zulu cause
became a common theme during the 1980s. In 1984 the king said
that 'some blacks in urban areas who want to disassociate
themselves from their brothers and sisters in the rest of KwaZulu'
should be 'cast out of our midst'. They were compared to witches,

'preying on our humanness, preying on our Zuluness, belittling our past, and making us ashamed of our present' (*City Press*, 30.09.84). At the 1986 Shaka Day celebrations, Goodwill warned these people in the following terms:

> *I also say this to you who are working with people and organisations alien to the great Zulu people – if you do not return to where you belong to work for your people, never imagine that you will escape detection for long (Natal Mercury, 25.09.86).*

On a national level Inkatha was being drawn increasingly into a network of nefarious and clandestine activities. While the Inkatha leadership maintained a rhetorical distance from the apartheid state, and most members were undoubtedly sincere in their rejection of apartheid, they were being funded by the organs of that state (police, foreign affairs and military intelligence). At the same time, Inkatha was being integrated more tightly into the security network's struggle against popular resistance and armed struggle. This new thrust coincided with the 1987 appointment of Jac Buchner as Natal Midlands chief of the security police. Buchner, involved in the creation of the 'Askaris' (turned ANC operatives), took command of the KwaZulu Police in 1989 (see Maré, 1989; LRC, 1991).

Buchner arrived in Pietermaritzburg in November 1987 shortly after the extensive and escalating outbreak of violence often related to an Inkatha recruitment drive in the Natal Midlands. He saw his task, and that of the police in general, as being to 'restore the rightful authority of the chiefs and indunas, the legal representatives of the KwaZulu government. These people happened to be Inkatha leaders as well' (quoted in Kentridge, 1990:208-9). His views on 'tradition', on Zulu ethnicity ('The ANC doesn't represent the whites, or the Zulus, whose leaders are their king and the KwaZulu cabinet under Buthelezi'), and on the status of the ANC, UDF and Cosatu, suited him for his subsequent role as KwaZulu commissioner of police.

While he claimed in 1989 that the KwaZulu police force was a neutral body, he also said that 'we have no real fear of the ANC or the SACP' and that 'it is more peaceful in this territory, a blend of urban and rural living, than anywhere else in South Africa' – this after some 3 000 people had been killed in the region between 1987 and 1989 (quoted LRC, 1991:42).

By the time that FW de Klerk made his historic announcement in February 1990, Inkatha and KwaZulu leaders were already engaged in formal consultation with the government. This centred on the relevance of their federal proposal, encapsulated in the Indaba constitution, and on other 'obstacles in the way of negotiations' (including the release of Mandela and other political prisoners).

Then, in December 1991, the latest chapter in the manipulation of ethnicity started when Buthelezi refused to attend the Convention for a Democratic South Africa talks unless recognition was given to the special status of the 'Zulu nation' through an invitation to King Goodwill Zwelethini to participate as the representative of seven million Zulus. Buthelezi's absence from the Codesa talks signified Inkatha's retreat into the ethnic and regional fortress it had so assiduously worked to create during the 1980s – then as a 'stepping stone', now as a kraal behind a moat.

Cultural distinctiveness and a Zulu past

De Wet Nel, quoted above, referred to the pride that was said to distinguish the various African ethnic groups in South Africa for over a century. King Goodwill, in the case of 'the Zulus', expressed that 'ethnic continuity' in the following way:

> *The unity between the Prince of KwaPhindangene, Prince Mangosuthu Buthelezi and myself symbolise(s) the unity of the nation. And what the Prince of KwaPhindangene has said today about the genius of King Shaka and his statesmanship in founding a vast Zulu empire, is a genius which I know is still at work in the hearts and minds of all Zulus (GS, 24.09.86).*

In Goodwill's conception, two of the elements in the definition and legitimation of ethnicity suggested earlier are brought together in mutual reinforcement: the existence of a distinct group, and the mobilisation of the past to give credibility to that social identity. However, Goodwill often goes beyond these elements, expressing a quasi-mystical element of 'genius' or 'wisdom' specific to Zulu people.

The first set of these symbols of legitimation that Inkatha functions with (the existence of a distinct group) arises from the pre-colonial history of the region and the manner in which capitalism penetrated this part of south-east Africa. This rested on the maintenance and exploitation – through taxes and labour – of the African homestead as a productive unit (see Guy, 1990). The second set of symbols (mobilisation of the past to give credence to the present) are drawn from the formation of the ANC in 1912 and its pre-eminence as the national liberation movement.

It is regionalism, and more specifically the immediate pre-colonial and colonial regionally-distinctive history, that has made a population 'available' for ethnic mobilisation and ethnic confirmation in Natal (for a discussion of the outlines of a strong regionalism, see Beall et al, 1986). The uneven penetration and development of capitalism in Natal articulated with the centralising dynamics within pre-capitalist society (the Shakan kingdom and its successors). As a result, it was only in the last quarter of the 19th century that the Zulu kingdom was defeated and Zululand (north of the Tukela river) incorporated into the colony. The 1906 Bambatha rebellion in Natal has been characterised as the last resistance against the spread of capitalism in South Africa (Marks, 1970).

What notion of history?

Buthelezi's use of history (and he, through his speeches, has undertaken most of the historical interpretation for Inkatha) is multi-dimensional:

• there is a history that gives credibility to his personal role as

'condensation' of what it means to be 'Zulu' (he is in the royal lineage; his forefathers served as 'prime ministers', etc);
- there is a history that justifies involvement in apartheid structures, such as the bantustans (KwaZulu existed long before apartheid, and Buthelezi's bantustan chief ministership is merely a confirmation of a post that he held in any case);
- there is a history that places the king at the head of a 'nation', of which he is the symbol and the personification;
- there is the history of the subject members of the nation who participated in heroic deeds, owed allegiance to a central authority figure, and who behaved in particular ways;
- and finally, there is the history that concerns me most here, that of 'the past' and the origins of an ethnic identity that serves contemporary purposes, and is present in each of the other dimensions of the use of history.

In Buthelezi's presentation of this history, the 'Zulu nation' was always already in existence, something that 'Zulus' were born into. It owed nought to apartheid (a white-designed system also based on the 'imagined' existence of 'the Zulu nation', along with nine other African 'nations'). Anyone who denied the existence of this Zulu nation became the object of volatile threats and strong language. In a recent memorandum delivered during the South Africa visit of Australian Foreign Affairs Minister Gareth Evans, Buthelezi said that 'In dealing with KwaZulu the South African government was dealing with *a reality that history structured*', and that the 'homeland framework' was imposed 'on what was an existing Zulu nation' (BS, 12.06.91, emphasis added). Frequently, and more regularly since the 'Zulu nation' has been discussed in national forums such as Codesa, it has been suggested that this social unit 'has existed since time immemorial'.

A specific perception of history underlies this use of 'the past' within Zulu ethnicity. History, in this case, is seen as an active agency that intervenes in the present – to confirm, to teach, to trample and to structure the foundations of the present. 'History', therefore, cannot be defied. Because it has already been, it cannot be altered. What it has destined cannot be undone, and the 'Zulu nation cannot be wished away'.

A very good, if slightly extreme, example of the repeated use of the term 'history', can be found in a speech Buthelezi gave on Shaka Day in 1988 (BS, 24.09.88). In this seven-page speech he used the notion of 'history' no less than 30 times. Zulus were a product of history, and participated with history to create a new South Africa; history taught, and still teaches; 'history tramples on tyranny and...history moves to uphold justice'; history has 'prepared a place for us'; history is 'guiding us' to a destiny; and so on.

In a revealing study aimed at tracing the utilisation of history 'as a source of political legitimation', Paul Forsyth (1989) wrote that Buthelezi's use of history probably exceeds that of 'any other career politician'. As I have argued earlier, this use of 'the past' is one of the defining elements of ethnic mobilisation.

Other examples of South African politicians who have relied to such a large extent on history also emerged from attempts at ethnic group formation – Afrikaners, the pathetic attempts by politicians in the Ciskei to create and utilise a history (see Peires, 1987), and the more recent 'Boer' mobilisation (through, for example, the Afrikaner Weerstandsbeweging), come to mind.

The Ciskei example represents an extreme case in the recent history of attempts to create an artificial 'past'. This bantustan was, even in terms of apartheid policy, an artificial unit. As Peires commented (1987:1): 'The Ciskei is unique among South African homelands in that it has absolutely no basis in any ethnic, cultural or linguistic fact whatsoever'. A 'Ciskei nation had to be created from scratch'. This was attempted through finding 'holy shrines', ancestries 'worth boasting about', and the invocation of 'fallen heroes...to give Ciskei nationhood some sort of time-depth'. In the absence of the availability of people to respond to something that had a basis in history, 'Sebe chose an ideology of "Ciskeian nationalism", thus committing himself to the invention of a wholly novel and therefore bogus ethnicity' (Peires, 1987:22).

In Buthelezi's case, he had a population available for ethnic mobilisation. When he became chief executive officer of the Zulu Territorial Authority (ZTA), the forerunner to the KwaZulu bantustan, he described the event in terms of regaining the power

the 'Zulu nation' had lost through defeat by the British in the 19th
century. His task was to restore 'pride' and 'Zulu national consciousness' through leading the ZTA (quoted Forsyth, 1989:52), a
phrase that later became a reference to a 'Zulu renaissance'. There
was no doubt in his mind that such an entity as the 'Zulu nation'
existed – it just needed to be revealed again. A reading of the early
KwaZulu Legislative Assembly (KLA) debates confirms that the
participants – chiefs and other 'tribal authority' represen- tatives –
held the same overarching common-sense idea of a 'nation'.

Within 'the past' that is used to confirm a 'Zulu nation' the
figure of Shaka looms large. Most of the relevant lineages are
traced back to the 'founding father' of the Zulu ethnic group,
while this Shaka displays all the attributes that have somehow
survived the past 170 years to find expression either in King
Goodwill, in Buthelezi, or in the 'nation'. This Shaka, of
Buthelezi's ideological creation,

> *that magnificent forefather of the Zulu nation, already saw the*
> *new South Africa as inevitable even while he was putting the*
> *Zulu Kingdom together. Before he died he had visions of*
> *aeroplanes flying in the air carrying people, and he sent*
> *emissaries to go to Cape Town with instructions to go to Britain*
> *to see what there was to see and learn, so that the Zulu*
> *Kingdom could incorporate the best there was in its own life... I*
> *(Buthelezi) am not adding interpretations to historic events. I*
> *am telling it as it was. I trace my own ancestry back to the very*
> *founders of KwaZulu. From my mother's knee onwards I grew*
> *up being seeped (sic) in what it meant to be a Zulu and what*
> *Zuluness meant to a man and a woman (BS, 18.01.92).*

Shaka features in this version, and in the many variations on the
theme during Shaka Day speeches, not for historical accuracy or
analysis, but for what it adds to Buthelezi and his project as an
ethnic mobiliser. Forsyth's study concluded that

> *Buthelezi's appeals to a range of histories have been successful*
> *in political terms, not because of their inherent truth, but*

> *because of the skills which he has shown in suiting his historical discourses to his political purposes (Forsyth, 1989:abstract).*

That is how ideology operates – by telling a story which provides a plausible explanation of what exists, what was, and what is desirable and plausible. 'Inherent truth' may have little to do with it. It is the receptivity of a population to these calls, the availability of people to be so mobilised, that is important. Such availability does not imply passivity, but draws attention to the historical specificity and socio-economic conditions within which such a 'story' is told.

In Natal and KwaZulu, large numbers of people have lived their lives as Zulus, even if they have different ideas as to the content of that notion (see Sitas, 1988). The appeals and interpretations of 'Zuluness' have been successful precisely 'because they have used emotive appeals to the "nation" to appeal to a popular perception of Zulu ethnic identity which exists in Natal and KwaZulu' (Forsyth, 1989:197). In addition, the regional Zulu-speaking population has lived a socially precarious and deprived existence where promises of material improvement or the means of survival have been major factors in acceptance or rejection of mobilising calls.

Allegiance to the 'Zulu nation' – measured through membership of Inkatha – could determine access to resources. Inkatha claimed total representation of 'Zuluness' in the first years after its formation in 1975. It was also the sole party in the bantustan government. Those who sought to politicise and mobilise Zulu ethnicity also controlled pensions, land allocation and education; signed work-seekers' permits; and approved bottle store licences. There were and are, therefore, both 'positive' and 'negative' inducements to accept the specific version of ethnic identity into which Buthelezi organises people, and that is given form in Inkatha. The former are found in the pride, self-worth, solidarity, and discovery of what an illustrious past can offer; the latter lie in an instrumental acceptance of the specific Inkatha version of that identity due to the material and political pressures (sometimes extremely violent) applied to large sections of the regional population.

Authority, or what is a Zulu?

'Brothers born of warrior stock': that is what King Goodwill Zwelethini called Zulus when he addressed 'the Zulu nation and...all South Africans' in May 1991. This speech drew together many themes in the political mobilisation of 'Zulus'. The king placed himself 'aloof from politics' and 'above party politics'; conflated KwaZulu, his person, and 'my father's people' ('I am the Zulu nation'); and linked the issue of 'cultural weapons' to one of the most frequent characteristic attributed to Zuluness: 'The call to ban the bearing of cultural weapons by Zulus is an insult to my manhood. It is an insult to the manhood of every Zulu man' (GS, 26.05.91).

This idea of 'manhood' permeates the vision of the essence of Zuluness. That essence is tied to men – to men as warriors, as leaders, as primary bearers of what constitutes this ethnic identity, as carriers of the lineage from Shaka to Buthelezi. In this lineage, the role of women is acknowledged only as bearers of men. As Cherryl Walker put it, mothers are never mothers of mothers! Women are placed within the warrior tradition, but as the bearers of warriors. Women reproduce, but are never themselves within 'the past':

> We the mothers of this part of South Africa have in our inner
> beings, in our deep wisdom and in our very blood, the lessons
> that history has taught us. We are the mothers of a great
> warrior nation... (IBS, 20.05.90).

The institute of chiefship is an essential element in this masculine and hierarchically-ordered view of 'Zuluness'. In one of his speeches, Buthelezi spoke of chiefs as having a 'depth of commitment...to each other as Zulu brothers born out of Zulu warrior stock', a commitment that cannot be understood by those who call for the disbanding of KwaZulu (BS, 13.09.90). Elsewhere he referred to chiefs as the pillars on which the 'Zulu nation' stands. The chiefs are also sanctioned by history: 'You the Zulu Amakhosi (chiefs) know that history lives on through you', Buthelezi said (BS, 13.09.90).

Over the years, the role of chiefs within the Inkatha-controlled regional administration of KwaZulu has not conflicted with the policy of the central state. The Bantu Authorities Act of 1951 committed the apartheid state to base its policy towards Africans on these remnants from the past. The 1959 Promotion of Bantu Self-Government Act confirmed that commitment and established the principle of ethnic fragmentation of the African people. It was under these two Acts that Buthelezi became a chief and then chief minister of KwaZulu. When the Zulu Territorial Authority was established in 1970 its constitution, as in the case of the other bantustans, provided for chiefs or their representatives to predominate. This remained so, even after the first elections to the KwaZulu Legislative Assembly were held in 1978. Before this, the KLA was made up solely of regional authority representatives (chiefs or their alternatives).

In 1974 Buthelezi wrote in the KwaZulu Government Diary, an official publication, that

We will preserve the traditional system of Chieftainship in KwaZulu and re-affirm our constitutional relationship with the Paramount Chief and will build our future state with due regard to our cultural heritage and traditions adapted and fructified by the ideals of Western civilization and democracy and modern scientific principles (quoted Maré and Hamilton, 1987:89).

In 1975 Buthelezi called chiefs and tribal authorities the base of government in KwaZulu, and repeated a frequently-voiced call for 'adequate' payment of chiefs. In 1976 salary increases were demanded as 'substantial salaries' would 'prevent chiefs from falling into temptation as the political situation is full of intrigue' (*KLAD*, 8, 1976:69).

The KwaZulu Chiefs and Headmen Act (1974) made it clear

that maintenance of control over the ethnically defined regional population remained an important function of chiefs. The tenor of debates in the KLA has supported this view. Buthelezi did not hesitate to use the Act against the rebellious Chief Mhlabunzima Maphumulo, who led anti-Inkatha moves in the late-1970s. Buthelezi's address to a meeting of KwaZulu chiefs in 1989 made it clear that he perceived this sort of defection from the ranks of the pliant Zulu chiefs in a most serious light, and as an assault on the symbolic role of chiefs within the 'Zulu nation':

> *We have come to close ranks and to rejoice in our unity and to tell Chief Maphumulo to go to hell. We must do what needs to be done... We have a duty to flush out anything that in any way undermines the unity and solidarity of our people (quoted in Survey, 1989/90:510).*

Maphumulo was assassinated after he joined the ANC-aligned Congress of Traditional Leaders of South Africa (Contralesa) in 1989.

The Indaba constitution drawn up in 1986, which still reflects an influential perspective on regional government for Natal and KwaZulu, made provision for chiefs to play an important role. It provided for a 'council of chiefs', for 'tribal authority' to remain as a form of local government, and for the existence of 'tribal police'.

Buthelezi did not always find it smooth sailing with the chiefs, many of whom were suspicious of his motives in the early 1970s. In 1975, Buthelezi attempted to shift the formal centre of power in KwaZulu from the KLA to the Inkatha movement. This would have taken power away from the chiefs, who dominated in the KLA. Buthelezi did not fully trust the chiefs at the time, as they owed a considerable amount of allegiance to the king. Within Inkatha, chiefs became necessary functionaries, with important organisational and symbolic roles. But Inkatha's leadership was firmly controlled by the small, but ambitious, trading class and some professionals (see Maré and Hamilton, 1987:59-60). In the KLA, on the other hand, chiefs had the potential to exercise political power independently of Buthelezi.

Finally, Buthelezi had to back down on the issue of Inkatha supremacy over the KLA. This conflict explains the chiefs' initial reluctance to participate in Inkatha recruitment drives. Later, this changed when it became obvious to chiefs that their future, in an increasingly precarious social and political world, lay with Buthelezi – himself the big chief, Ndunankulu, chief among chiefs.

One of the few exceptions, in this world of male and 'traditional' authority, provided the general rule. In 1992, Dr Sibongile Zungu won a Durban Supreme Court battle to become the first female Zulu chief. Her husband, the previous chief, had died in a car accident in 1989, after which relatives and male clan members began the battle to keep her out of the chiefship. They attempted to 'marry' her to her husband's brother; called on 'traditional practices' to ensure that he became chief; and argued that it was 'entirely unknown among the Zulu people for a woman to be appointed as chief of a tribe' (*Sunday Tribune*, 05.04.92).

Inkatha's Women's Brigade provides an important illustration of the role of women within Inkatha and within the 'Zulu nation'. Hassim has noted that the Brigade's mobilising appeal is directed at 'mothers' concerned about their children 'in the context of poverty, ignorance and disease'; their children and education; and at the danger of their children being attracted into the ANC fold (Hassim, 1992:21-22). The Women's Brigade (WB), formed in 1977 and placed as 'one of the President's (Buthelezi's) own arms of activity' in 1980, confirmed the role of women as 'home-makers'. As former WB chairperson Abbie Mchunu said in 1985, 'there are special virtues God gave us as women in order to be effective home-managers and mothers, ie patience, tenderness of heart and insight' (quoted in Hassim, 1992:12-13). But, noted Hassim,

> *the conservative discourse that emerges within Inkatha has not merely been imposed by men from above, it is a discourse produced out of a resonance of ideas of motherhood and family that are held by women themselves and which fit into their daily reality (1992:13).*

71

This position has been reinforced by the political role of the youth since 1976, which has threatened values and institutions such as family structures.

Buthelezi's wife, Irene Thandekila Buthelezi, has called on women to restore and maintain not only the values of family and parental authority but also to safeguard wider administrative authority threatened by the youth: 'When bands of youth take it upon themselves to crush their local authorities, whether they be *Amakhosi* or township personnel, say no and say no in such a way that the youth are stopped' (IBS, 20.05.90).

The Inkatha version of the Zulu ethnic group sanctions male-dominated gender relations, and a hierarchy of authority in which the chiefs stand anointed by tradition. But there are many other elements explicit and implicit in this mobilisation of ethnicity. These include obedience to the law; wisdom; bravery; patience; non-violence and yet a fearful wrath if KwaZulu, Zulus, the king or Buthelezi are insulted; humanism; and an approach to life with not a 'vestige of racism'. In a most fearsome speech, King Goodwill pulled together many of these attributes to draw a clear line around the boundaries of the Zulu ethnic group, as mobilised behind his and Buthelezi's leadership:

> *Not only do Zulus have valour, not only are they indomitable and not only are they prudent, but Zulus have a quality superior to any of these, as great as these qualities are. The final strength of our Zulu nation has always been wisdom. It is wisdom that led our illustrious Kings and their warriors to conquer and to incorporate.*

He then attacked the UDF, Cosatu and the ANC for 'undermining our national unity as a Zulu people', repeating the frequent theme of 'conquering to incorporate':

> *I command you to eliminate from your midst all those disgusting usurpers of our dignity without one shred of malice in your beings… Go out my people, conquer evil, but never lose your humanity and never degrade the humanity of those you*

conquer. Rout them out only to make them one of us. Thrash them, if necessary, only to purge them into becoming better Zulus (GS, 16.06.86).

Inkatha is 'the nation'

The idea that there had always been a Zulu nation, which was being confirmed through restoration of the past under the leadership of Buthelezi, initially centred on the existence of the Zulu Territorial Authority (from 1970-72) and subsequently the KwaZulu Legislative Assembly. These were presented either as structures of apartheid that could be used to overthrow the system, or as acknowledgements of the Zulu nation's re-awakening.

From 1975, however, the idea of a pre-existing nation was given additional organised form in the Inkatha movement. The KwaZulu bantustan was too fragile a base on which to construct a community like the nation. However, KwaZulu was not discarded as an administrative and ideological form for the nation; rather, it was provided with a back-up.

Inkatha is first and foremost an example of politicised ethnicity. Its symbols serve to mobilise a 'constituency' which finds expression through branch and regional structures, women's and youth organisations, events, a variety of media, museums, styles of dress, education, etc. These symbols, in turn, define the Zulu ethnic identity that they at the same time reflect.

The constituency is primarily formed through 'Zuluness'. And it is membership of the organised constituency, Inkatha, that implies acceptance of 'Zuluness'. These appeals for people to recognise themselves as 'Zulus' at times achieve their potency not only through the availability of the past, but also through the existence of an enemy, real or created. The enemy, the 'other', helps to define 'us' as the 'Zulu nation'. The three major characteristics of an ethnic group are exemplified by accepting a Zulu identity (and, in this politicised version, by belonging to Inkatha). Cultural distinctiveness and a sense of an historical continuity are presented as inseparable. And 'the past' is expressed in the present through cultural events, artifacts, modes of behaviour, norms and memorials.

The past is mobilised both through the Inkatha movement, and also a more generalised notion of nationhood that originated in the time of Shaka in the first quarter of the 19th century. Inkatha's 1975 constitution claimed a continuity with the first Inkatha, formed under King Solomon in the 1920s (see Cope, 1986; Marks, 1986). The 1975 constitution was headed as follows: 'Founded in 1928 – by King Solomon ka Dinuzulu', while the movement itself was initially linked to the 'Zulu nation' ('Inkatha kaZulu') rather than the wider 'Inkatha Yesizwe' (of the nation) which it became soon after.

The choice of the name, Inkatha, not only referred back to the movement in the 1920s, but drew on the symbolism it implied:

In choosing to revive Inkatha, Chief Buthelezi was exploiting a solemn symbol of unity in Zulu culture. Among the most sacred articles of the Zulu, of which the king was a custodian, is the inkatha, a sacred coil symbolising the unity of the people, the circular power of which is believed to be able to round up all traitors and disaffected subjects and join them together with the rest of the 'nation' in affection for the king (Mzala, 1988:117).

Matters went further than that in rooting the organisation in 'tradition' and in the region: chiefs were seen as central in recruitment for Inkatha, even if they were not given the same constitutional weight that they had in the KLA, and were reprimanded in the KwaZulu Legislative Assembly for their initial lack of enthusiasm for the new movement (eg *KLAD*, 7, 1975:921); and Inkatha branches were planned to coincide with the areas of tribal authorities.

As discussed above, the integration of chiefs into Inkatha was not a smooth process. But if 'the past' was to bestow legitimacy on Buthelezi, he had to draw chiefs in, even to the extent of using fairly direct threats to their fate as 'traditional' leaders. The chiefs' 'traditional' role confirms his own 'traditional' role: 'I was the traditional Prime Minister to my first cousin, King Cyprian for 16

74

years, long before there was any KwaZulu Legislative Assembly'
(*Sunday Tribune*, 06.11.83); and

> *I do not owe my political power to the KwaZulu Legislative*
> *Assembly or to Pretoria. King Shaka never owed his political*
> *eminence to any colonial power. The solidarity of the Zulu*
> *people was not dependent on white-created institutions when*
> *they defeated the might of the British Army (Sunday Times,*
> *16.01.83).*

The regular gatherings of chiefs, under the leadership of Buthelezi
as minister in charge of 'authority affairs' in the KwaZulu cabinet,
served to confirm a Zulu past and an ethnic tradition, safeguarded
only within Inkatha and under the leadership of Buthelezi. In
1990, for example, Buthelezi guided discussion by the chiefs
through a memorandum in which he warned that they were
engaged in a war where the youth and Contralesa were launching
campaigns. At this meeting Buthelezi reassured the chiefs of their
future security and confirmed their role within the 'nation':

> *We must... begin this meeting with a new determination starting*
> *to burn within us. It is a determination that must see us leave*
> *this meeting later on with an anger that rejects the many bad*
> *developments in our areas of responsibility. It is a*
> *determination to now be more decisive in our actions to rid us*
> *of these bad developments. And it must be a determination that*
> *gives allegiance to our Zulu nation and all that our forefathers*
> *did to deliver this great nation to us and to history. It is a*
> *determination also to reaffirm our loyalty to our King (BS,*
> *23.03.90).*

Initially, Buthelezi saw all members of the 'Zulu nation' as
members of Inkatha:

> *... all members of the Zulu nation are automatically members of*
> *Inkatha if they are Zulus. There may be people who are inactive*
> *members as no one escapes being a member as long as he or*
> *she is a member of the Zulu nation (KLAD, 5, 1975:134).*

75

In the absence of any clear opposition, both political and in terms of defining a Zulu ethnicity outside of Inkatha, this all-encompassing nature of membership was understandable in the early days of Inkatha's existence. Enemies, the 'other', were at that time most frequently represented as 'Indians', 'white liberals', 'Xhosas', or the central government. By the 1980s, however, with growing internal, organised and alternative opposition to apartheid, Inkatha had to recognise an 'enemy within' which had to be exorcised. It had to acknowledge that there were not only ethnic outsiders but also *traitors* to the imagined community of all Zulu-speakers as well.

On several occasions, King Goodwill made it clear that Zulu traitors existed, and that they should be brought back into the fold through a 'Zulu renaissance' or chastisement. 'We have always rooted out Zulus who turn against Zulus and in so doing we have kept our honour. It does not shame the whole nation when traitors emerge amongst us as a people'.

The problem, for the king, lay in allowing the traitors to 'go about their hideous divisive work unchecked'. Two evils had to be exorcised: the one involved Zulus who did not accept the notion of 'nationhood' (or Zulu ethnicity) propagated by Inkatha, and who did not respect 'my uncle, the Chief Minister' or the KwaZulu government; the other was the organisational onslaught 'that comes from without to creep into our midst to do the hideous things that are now being done amongst you'.

Against both these attacks, Goodwill called on true 'Zulus' to revenge the insult against himself as symbol of 'national (Zulu) unity'.

This speech, delivered on Soweto Day, 16 June 1986, spelled out vividly that there could be no organisations or ideologies within 'Zuludom' which posed alternatives to Inkatha. Unity in struggle lay through Inkatha, or through being 'Zulu', as Goodwill put it in this speech (see Maré and Hamilton, 1987:218-21, for an extended discussion of this idea).

Goodwill's comments demonstrate the manner in which the boundaries of an ethnic group are constantly changing or being reinforced through new strands in the mix of elements that make up that identity. This has occurred more recently in the Afrikaner ethnic group as well, where the boundaries of language and religion became inadequate. The redefinition of an 'Afrikaner' identity (now as *'Boer'*) depends on a new religion that defines 'mud races' as not fully human, and a political myth of origin that is tied to a separate political area (the old Boer Republics, the Volkstaat, etc).

This redefinition is aimed at fellow 'Afrikaners' as much as it is at a wider population of more 'traditional' enemies. The language used by King Goodwill – of traitors and infiltrators – also characterises that of the Afrikaans-speaking far right as it seeks to mobilise a new Afrikaner ethnicity.

Mobilising the past

Nationalism, unlike ethnicity, insists on political sovereignty within national boundaries. But territory can also be used to draw spatial boundaries around an ethnic group.

Once Buthelezi and Inkatha had gained control over the KwaZulu bantustan, they attempted to give it an existence beyond the one allocated by apartheid, defining the territory as the home of the 'Zulu nation'. But in 1982, ironically, a threat to a large part of the new 'Zulu kingdom' was launched by the National Party government. This involved a deal between the conservative kingdom of Swaziland and the South African government which allocated large sections of northern Zululand (the Ingwavuma area) and most of the KaNgwane bantustan to Swaziland.

There was considerable speculation over the reasons for the deal at the time. Here it is sufficient to note that landlocked Swaziland would have benefited from access to a potential port at Kosi Bay; and the South African government would have shed responsibility for another ethnically-defined population, in the way that it had already done through bantustan 'independence'. The deal would also have made the Swaziland government more active in combatting the movement of ANC members through its territory.

The ethnic dimension was an essential feature of this proposed 'land deal', not only on the part of the government, but also from all others directly involved. Those living in the Ingwavuma district are Thonga, who had paid tribute to Shaka briefly in the early 19th century and later to Cetshwayo. More recently, Thonga men had developed a history of 'ethnic fence jumping' in response to a labour market they believed was more receptive to the employment of Zulus than Thongas. The core ideas of Thonga identity, such as the language and status of women within the family, were maintained by Thonga women as the men adopted a 'Zulu' identity (see above and Webster, 1991).

In opposing the proposed land deal, Buthelezi and Inkatha showed little interest in the relative fluidity of ethnic identities in the region. Rather, they attempted to demonstrate that even if the Ingwavuma people were not 'true Zulus' then at least they had bowed to the 'Zulu nation' in the past. As proof of the Zulu presence in Ingwavuma, Buthelezi claimed that King Dingane was buried in the district, 'adding weight to the correctness of Zulu control' from Ulundi. At the end of May 1982, he announced that a tombstone would be built to Dingane 'to emphasise the Zulu presence'. He warned at a press conference that he would 'not be at all surprised' if fighting over the issue broke out between Zulus and Swazis in hostels, mines and townships (see Maré and Hamilton, 1987; DSG/SARS, 1982). In this way, he extended the symbols of Zulu ethnicity, in this case through King Dingane, to the territory of the Tembe-Thonga.

There are other examples of Buthelezi's attempts to extend ethnically-defined territory: the south of Natal, where the competition for people and land was with the Transkei; and the north-eastern Orange Free State, where Radio Zulu broadcasts and calls for the provision of Zulu-language schools in the region reflect but two of the attempts to extend territory.

Within the heartland of KwaZulu, Buthelezi and Inkatha have 'captured' monuments and historical sites to define territory, both physically and symbolically. Resistance to such appropriation by Inkatha has led to violence and death: the 1983 clash between students at the University of Zululand and Inkatha supporters over the commemoration of the death of Cetshwayo was a good example of this. Students were unwilling to let Inkatha on to the campus for this celebration, while Buthelezi's would not allow 'no-go' areas for Inkatha within his territory.

As expected within a 'warrior tradition', battle sites feature prominently in the commemorations of a 'Zulu' past. In 1981, for example, Buthelezi announced the intention of the newly-formed KwaZulu Monuments Foundation to restore no fewer than 74 historic battlefields (*Sunday Times*, 23.08.81).

At Ondini, near Ulundi the capital of KwaZulu, the royal residence of King Cetshwayo has been restored and a museum of Zulu culture constructed at a cost of R500 000. As Wright and Mazel noted in an article on museums in Natal and KwaZulu, 'history is not a set of facts about the past but, rather, a set of ideas about the past held in the present' (1988:1). Museums, and other representations of the past are, therefore, important in the use of the past to create group boundaries. They play an important part in shaping perceptions of 'shared experiences'. Wright and Mazel argued that the museums at Ulundi fulfil several functions: they 'assert the legitimacy of KwaZulu as a political entity', through portraying 'the KwaZulu polity as the "natural" successor state of the Zulu kingdom'; and the museums and their displays 'assert the legitimacy of the present KwaZulu leadership' – both the king, presented as the obvious successor in an unbroken line from Shaka, and Buthelezi, presented as a 'natural' leader of Zulus and through connections with the royal family (1988:9). The dominant message of the displays is of 'social discipline and order', to the exclusion of struggle and disunity over what constituted a Zulu identity.

More recently, Buthelezi has cast the net to include 'Zulus' even wider, throughout Southern Africa. In a Shaka Day speech in 1991 (BS, 21.09.91) he referred to various 'Zulu' thrusts that produced united peoples. Soshangane, for example, 'took with him some thousand Zulu warriors who also conquered where they went, and who also united wherever they conquered' in Mozambique. In the same way he traced the unifying thrust into Zimbabwe and Zambia:

> *All the Ndebele people (in Zimbabwe) know that they are one people with us. All the Shangane people (in Mozambique) know that they are one people with us. All the Angoni people (in Zambia) know that they are one people with us.*

According to recent reports, Inkatha delegations have ventured beyond the borders of South Africa to 'recruit' and establish links with 'Zulus' in Southern African countries (see, for example, *New Nation*, 03.04.92 and 10.04.92).

There are many examples of the events that have been created to reaffirm a Zulu past and present identity: Shaka Day, the recently-revived Reed Dance ceremonies, the creation of a Zulu Monuments Commission and the commemoration of such events as the battle of Isandlwana are but a few of these.

Buthelezi had offered to organise the first Shaka Day in September 1954. While the ANC had wanted to 'establish an historical continuity between the alleged ideals of Shaka and those of the ANC', Buthelezi benefited from the public recognition and the presentation 'as a traditionalist whose support and allegiance lay with the Zulu King' (Forsyth, 1989:22). In 1971 the ZTA appealed to the South African government to declare a Shaka Day holiday in September, and Buthelezi claimed that 'all the tribes (in Natal and Zululand) were under Shaka's authority and nobody had any doubts that he was the founder of the Zulu nation' (quoted in Forsyth, 1989:56).

In October 1986 the South African Broadcasting Corporation (SABC) TV service released a ten-part series called 'Shaka Zulu'. In supporting the idea of the series, King Goodwill stated that the 'founder of the Zulu nation' should be saved from a Eurocentric and white perspective and judged 'in the context of African history as recounted by his people' (*Sunday Times*, 12.10.86). In the Shaka Zulu *Official Souvenir Brochure*, the SABC wrote that 'King Goodwill not only gave Faure (director of the series) the go-ahead, but also bestowed upon the project the blessing of the Zulu royal house, as well as their full support and cooperation'. Buthelezi's mother became music advisor, until her death during the filming of the series.

Historians also joined the fray. Carolyn Hamilton wrote that the 'Great Man' notion of history, propagated through the series and through Inkatha's discourse, 'is likely to produce passive actors in the present rather than active participants in the building of a new South Africa'. John Wright said that 'if history has shown us anything, it is that politicians use history to further their own ends, and Chief Buthelezi is a politician not a historian' (*Natal Mercury*, 30.09.86).

In December 1986 John Wright and I wrote an article dealing with the series as a political statement. Published in the Natal Sunday paper (*Sunday Tribune*, 07.12.86) under the title 'The Splice of Coincidence', the article argued that 'conflicting interest groups constantly raid the past for justification of their specific policies and practices'. In this case the interests of the state, through the SABC, and Inkatha coincided. Buthelezi, through government-created institutions, had established himself as the 'chief interpreter of "Zuluism" '. Both the SABC and Inkatha were 'propagating an ideology which underpins the authority of the present KwaZulu leadership on two counts':

- First, the series portrays the history of the Zulu kingdom as the history of the Zulu royal family. The common people in the film dance, sing, fight, ululate, and grovel in the dust before their leaders, but they do not emerge as having a history of their own.
- Second, the series portrays the Zulu kingdom as having been politically and socially united. There is nothing in it about the deep political divisions in Shaka's conquest state between the new Zulu leadership and the chiefdoms it had subordinated.

The overall effect of the series was to reinforce the

ideological argument that the Zulu royal house is the unquestioned 'traditional' ruler of all 'Zulu' people today... It also reinforces the ideological assertion that, but for a few troublemaking dissidents, all Zulu people today are united behind the KwaZulu leadership.

Dr Oscar Dhlomo, then KwaZulu minister of education and Inkatha secretary general, responded with an inaccurate and *ad hominem* attack, offering no alternative information or analysis except to deny our argument. Clearly the article had struck a very sensitive point, questioning some of the basic premises of Inkatha's argument as to its own legitimacy within ethnic mobilisation.

That sensitivity has also been manifest in Buthelezi's reaction to the publication of a book by an intellectual within the ANC, Mzala (1988). Buthelezi threatened distributors, and even libraries, in South Africa with legal action if they even stocked the book.

Mzala's book set out to explain the 'political behaviour' of Chief Buthelezi through 'an attentive survey of his political past, from the time of his incorporation into the institution of chieftaincy in 1953...' (1988:4). To determine what Buthelezi found offensive we need to undertake a similar 'attentive survey', not only of what Mzala wrote but also of its context. That involves the central role Buthelezi occupies, largely self-created but reproduced extensively by others, within the myth of origin of the 'Zulu nation' and its existence since 1975 through and in the Inkatha movement.

If that role is undermined, the whole house comes tumbling down – at least as far as Buthelezi is concerned. It is not only that Buthelezi self-consciously manipulates history. He actually lives what he claims to be. The myth and the man, and the movement that he represents and his own identity, are one. Deny the one (or the way in which it has been constructed) and you deny the other.

Buthelezi has always been most sensitive to claims that he was the creation of apartheid, or that he was tolerated by the apartheid state while many others were prosecuted and hounded, jailed or killed for their opposition to apartheid. He has argued that he owes his prominent position as 'prime minister to the Zulu king' not to apartheid but to his common lineage with the royal house and previous 'prime ministers'. He had no choice but to lead 'his' people within a territory that was consolidated by Shaka, the 'Zulu kingdom'.

Mzala tackled these two central arguments not as ideological

constructions but as factually inaccurate.
Mzala argues that it was

> *not automatic that Gatsha should become chief of the*
> *Buthelezis... Shepstone laid the foundations of the role of chiefs*
> *in the present-day bantustan policy, almost a hundred years*
> *before the National Party came into power and passed the*
> *Bantu Authorities Act of 1951... Those chiefs who refused to*
> *co-operate with Shepstone's administrative hierarchy were*
> *simply deposed and new ones appointed from the same tribe.*
> *This he did skillfully, selecting from the ranks of the traditional*
> *chiefs themselves or their half-brothers, exploiting the existing*
> *rivalry for positions among them (1988:27).*

Mzala traces the various incorporations of chiefs into colonial,
Union and apartheid administrations. He continues his onslaught,
not against Buthelezi as such, but against the institutionalisation of
chieftainship, separating the good traditionalists from the bad:

> *From 1927 onwards, no chief who held political views contrary*
> *to those of the government was confirmed in his position as*
> *'chief' by the Governor-General, irrespective of his hereditary*
> *right by African custom (1988:42).*

Mzala therefore claims that only government-approved chiefs were
allowed to run the bantustans, and denies that any 'genuine leader
supported the Bantu Authorities Act' (1988:51). This denies
Buthelezi the approval he claims from such people as Chief Albert
Luthuli and Nelson Mandela: 'all chiefs who valued honour' were
expected to follow Luthuli in refusing to be 'a servant of the racist
government' (1988:56). He seriously questions Buthelezi's
opposition to the imposition of tribal authorities. Instead he argues
that there was a long period of participation, albeit under pressure
from the state at specific moments, both in fighting for his own
chiefship and in proving his worth to the government.

It is in chapter six, however, that Mzala strikes at the heart of
Buthelezi's symbolic underpinnings: Mzala questions his claim to

the title of *mntwana* (or prince), as he was not the son of a king; to the role of 'premier', as it was not an 'hereditary title' as Buthelezi claims; and he accuses Buthelezi of being silent about the role his great-grandfather Mnyamana played ('he betrayed Dinuzulu') (1988:105). Mzala claims that the founder of the 'Buthelezi tribe' was a Sotho herbalist; and, finally, he argues that through placing himself effectively above the king, Buthelezi inverted Zulu history, and that this state of affairs was made possible only through the powers conferred on him by the state through the bantustan system (1988:113).

In this way Mzala, himself a Zulu and – oddly for a member of the ANC and SACP – supportive of a untainted tradition of Zuluness, struck at the core of Buthelezi's mobilisation of politicised Zulu ethnicity.

Control through ideas and force

The 1970s and 1980s witnessed massive social dislocation and collapse, brought on by the ravages of apartheid and a changing economy. The assault on the structures of apartheid through popular resistance did not spare Inkatha. The movement responded by taking control of as many areas of social life as possible. It called the areas which it controlled under the apartheid system 'liberated zones', and attempted to impose its domination under the banner of 'Zuluness' within these areas. The various terrains Inkatha conquered illustrate the use made of 'Zulu traditions' in the struggle for political power. Two of these involved education and police.

The educational arena is a powerful one in the socialisation of individuals into specific identities. In the South African context, however, African pupils had shown great scepticism about the education provided for them and, especially since 1976, rejected Bantu Education with such vigour that schooling came to a halt for many. Bantu Education could not fulfil any of the tasks that it set itself: it did not train pupils for employment, partly because unemployment was growing during the 1970s; it did not socialise them into a broad acceptance of the justness of the society they were to live in, where 'nations' were to find the political kingdom in 'homelands'.

When the KLA was granted phase two self-governing status in 1977 it set about 'abolishing Bantu Education' (claimed in 1978), and then introduced the 'Inkatha syllabus' into schools (it was only later that proponents became sensitive to the implications of this name, as protest mounted at what was seen to be party-political propaganda).

The syllabus was geared to call pupils into the Zulu ethnic group and accept those norms and values desirable to 'being Zulu'. Respect, acceptance of authority and discipline were central aspects of the syllabus.

An hour-long weekly period was devoted to the teaching of the syllabus and, while not examinable, it was to be enforced through regular reports to school inspectors by teachers (for background to the introduction of the syllabus, see Maré, 1988/9). Teaching material made available to teachers of 'Inkatha' consisted of 'documents like the constitution, various pamphlets on the aims and philosophy of Inkatha, presidential addresses, and so on', said education minister and Inkatha secretary general, Oscar Dhlomo (*KLAD*, 16, 1979:346). The Inkatha Syllabus Committee said that they were influenced, in drawing up the syllabus, by the problem

> *that many adults seem to hold divergent views and beliefs about Inkatha for various reasons. These are passed on to the youth and cloud the youths' minds. It is thus hoped that this syllabus together with its guide will clear many doubts and thus create unified ideas to match with the goals of Inkatha (Inkatha Syllabus Committee, 1978:2).*

Mdluli, in his analysis of the Zulu texts written to guide the teachers in teaching the syllabus, focused on some of its core ideas (1987). He noted the central position allocated to Buthelezi, not merely as chief minister, but as 'political leader of the Zulu'. *Ukuhlonipha* (respect) is, he argued, the central theme of the syllabus. It 'sanctions superiority based on sex, age and social position and reproduces the whole set of authoritarian and hierarchical relations found in Zulu society'. Respect of youth for elders, of woman for men (in the words of the syllabus, 'The woman knows that she is not equal to her husband'), of respect for all authority figures, and respect for the law, are all aspects of *ukuhlonipha* that are stressed.

Mdluli commented that the *Ubuntu-botho* (humanism) syllabus made it clear that Inkatha's aim was 'not to destroy Zulu nationalism in the struggle against apartheid, but to mobilise this nationalism as a launching base' (1987:70). The syllabus accepted that the building-blocks of South African society were ethnic groups.

This educational mobilisation coincided with the regional consolidation strategy that the movement was undertaking at the time, and personified the struggle for liberation in the figure of Buthelezi. Mdluli concluded that the syllabus strengthened the 'three ideological pillars' of Inkatha's appeal in the region, namely 'the tradition of Shaka and other "great" Zulu kings' which is continued in Inkatha; Inkatha 'as the continuation of the early ANC'; and Inkatha as the 'embodiment of Zulu cultural traditions and values' (*UbuZulu* or 'Zuluness').

Natal had been relatively isolated from the turmoil in schools that began in 1976. Buthelezi told a rally in Umlazi in 1977 that 'Our Zulu youth has shown consistent responsibility. They did not burn down our schools which we built ourselves and by which we raise ourselves' (quoted Maré and Hamilton, 1987:185). Minister Oscar Dhlomo boasted in 1979 that 'I haven't found any evidence of unrest relating to political factors' in KwaZulu schools. He claimed that this was the case because Bantu Education had been abolished in KwaZulu.

In 1977 a circular from the Department of Education and Training told circuit inspectors to allow principals to hold Inkatha Youth Brigade meetings in schools, which Buthelezi said was because the movement had kept unrest out of the region (see Maré and Hamilton, 1987:183).

The need for discipline, and specifically discipline through the Inkatha movement, was repeatedly linked to an ethnic identity, both in the Inkatha syllabus and in public pronouncements. In 1980 Buthelezi warned:

Inkatha as such has proved beyond any doubt to be the best instrument to sort out the problems of discipline and also the problem of lack of patriotism... (T)he reason why that (schools unrest) has in fact not taken off came about as a result of this discipline which Inkatha merely strengthens. In this region King Shaka was the first person to make us a disciplined people, and through the various traumas we have encountered as a people and where we have been split apart, I think Inkatha has been that instrument which sought to re-establish that discipline on which our nation operated at that time (KLAD, 18, 1980:356).

Shortly after this warning, a well-supported schools boycott took place in the KwaZulu-controlled KwaMashu township. Initially Buthelezi took refuge in the scapegoating of non-Zulus and blamed 'Xhosa' lawyers, 'foreign representatives', and so on for the boycott (Maré and Hamilton, 1987:185). He also claimed that the boycotts had been designed to 'denigrate' him personally.

Buthelezi threatened extreme violence, now that the discipline of the educational system had been shown to be illusory. Buthelezi claimed that there was a 'total onslaught' against Inkatha. He warned that once the 'political riff-raff' had been identified,

We will shake them and drive them out of our midst, and if they are not careful they may find that they run risks in what they do, one of which may be having their skulls cracked, as none of us can predict what form the anger they raise takes (quoted Maré and Hamilton, 1987:186).

This early case of the disciplinary powers of Inkatha – mass meetings were called and marching bands of Inkatha supporters assaulted adults and pupils – gave warning of the violence that was to accompany regional consolidation during the rest of the 1980s.

The formation of the KwaZulu police put Inkatha's warrior

tradition in uniform. The movement had not hesitated to demand and accept its 'own' police force for KwaZulu. In 1975 a KLA request was made that the central government be asked to hand over police power to the bantustan. But before that could happen, the bantustan needed greater powers than Pretoria had allocated it. In 1978, when these powers were granted, Jeffrey Mtetwa, KwaZulu minister of justice, said that the KLA 'not only aimed at taking over the police but would also ask Pretoria to give military training to tribal regiments' (*Natal Mercury*, 12.05.78).

This brought together the two most prominent aspects of Inkatha's direct and indirect organs of control (police and 'tribal regiments'). Chiefs, too, were mobilised to serve within a broad 'law and order' front. In 1974, for example, the KLA passed its own Zulu Chiefs and Headmen Act, repeating in many details the Native Administration Act of 1927 and its amendments. The KwaZulu Act stipulated that a chief or headman 'shall be entitled...to the loyalty, respect, support and obedience of every resident of the area for which he has been appointed'. It placed chiefs and their assistants as local representatives of the KwaZulu government in control of law and order enforcement, unrest, distribution of 'undesirable literature', and the prevention of 'unauthorised entry of any person into his area'.

After 1980, the police in many districts came under KLA control, while the establishment of a 'security section' and camouflaged 'riot police' were envisaged from early on. Considerable emphasis was made of tradition in the policing of the African inhabitants of Natal (Maré, 1989). It is not often that Buthelezi acknowledges the existence and operation of 'Zulu regiments'. In 1980, however, he was driven to do so in reaction to a newspaper report on the operation of 'mobs' during the KwaMashu schools boycotts. Buthelezi justified the presence of regiments and the sticks they carried as 'part and parcel of the Zulu national grouping, and the formation of regiments... (It) is part and parcel of Zulu tradition' (*KLAD*, 19, 1980:662).

Buthelezi, who is also KwaZulu minister of police, called the KwaZulu police 'my first bastion of defence against anything and everybody that mounts threats against the democracy which alone can set us free'. He addressed them as follows:

> *You now belong to the KwaZulu Police Force and I want you to infuse into our Police Force the sterling character and the great courage which has made the Zulu nation one of the great nations of the world. Right from the beginning of time for KwaZulu, we distinguished ourselves as human beings, powerful as warriors and wise as philosophers with an Ubuntu-Botho (humanism) approach to human problems... (T)here is a vast strength of Zuluness in the society around you, strengthening you and supporting you (BS, 21.01.87).*

Both education and policing were part of the drive for ethnic mobilisation through Inkatha. They intersected as well – if education failed in establishing 'unified ideas' then the police would be there to ensure that 'traitors' did not threaten the political existence of Inkatha. Inkatha has perceived such a threat in the working class in particular, a stratum of society that potentially cuts across the organisation of *politicised* ethnicity.

Disciplining the working class

In a survey of union members undertaken by Eddie Webster in 1975, only 19% named Buthelezi as a leader 'present or past' who could 'improve the position of African workers' (Luthuli, Natal-based president of the ANC before its banning, obtained 44% and Mandela 10%). However, Webster noted that 87% saw Buthelezi 'as their leader' (Webster, 1987:29-29).

It is not clear to what extent this reflected an acceptance of a specifically 'Zulu' political context, or whether it was simply an acknowledgement that the only avenue for open politics, without intense harassment, was bantustan political activity.

While Buthelezi remained consistent in his support for the legal recognition of trade unions for African workers, Inkatha simultaneously brought the conservative influence of the ideology of 'Zuluness' into the field of labour. This created few problems while the unions in the region were struggling to survive. They were weak and concentrated on factory-floor strength rather than political opposition to the state during the 1970s. In addition, in Natal the unions were sensitive to the powerful politics of Inkatha, and to its mobilisation of 'Zulus'. It was argued that workers could be members of both Inkatha and a union, as they catered for different spheres of life.

This stand-off changed drastically with the political direction followed by Inkatha in the 1980s, and with developments within the union movement itself. Inkatha had held the dream that unions would join it, and constitutional provision was made for such an eventuality, even if the envisaged representation was minor. But the relationship between Inkatha and the emerging unions became one of deep suspicion. Inkatha was wary of all mobilisation that fell outside of its control, while the unions were equally suspicious of all politics that was perceived to be part of 'the system'. From the end of the 1970s Inkatha leaders began hinting at moving into the labour field in its own right.

The Federation of South African Trade Unions (Fosatu) had been formed in 1979, with only 20 000 paid-up members, and included a block of unions from Natal which had been organised under the umbrella of the Trade Union Advisory Co-ordinating Council. An uneasy co-existence between Inkatha and Fosatu seemed possible, with each organisation stating that dual membership was permissible (Morris, 1986; Maré and Hamilton, 1987). However, with the formation of the Congress of South African Trade Unions (Cosatu) in 1985, the possibility of dual allegiances disappeared.

Inkatha had never been able to convince any credible union to affiliate to it, and this possibility disappeared completely with the launch of Cosatu. Inkatha then moved ahead with plans to establish a union, the United Workers Union of South Africa (Uwusa), launched on May Day 1986 at the same venue that Cosatu had chosen six months earlier. With a great deal of show Buthelezi landed in a helicopter in the rugby stadium, while supporters carried a coffin with the name of the Cosatu president written on it. Buthelezi stated that Uwusa was in opposition to the ANC and Cosatu, thereby placing choices of exclusive allegiance before the Natal working class.

Here I will refer to only three examples of the manner in which Inkatha brought ethnicity into the labour field – two from mining and the third from agriculture. In the field of labour recruitment 'Zulu tradition' continued to play a role, as it did in the 1910s (see Marks, 1986:33-34) and 1920s (see Cope, 1986:322). Buthelezi maintained a close relationship with the mining industry in South Africa during the 1970s and 1980s, largely through the recruiting organisation of the Chamber of Mines, The Employment Bureau of Africa (TEBA).

TEBA had, from the second half of the 1970s, focused attention on an internal market for labour after the independence of Mozambique and other Southern African disturbances had affected the smooth flow of mine labour. In 1981, for example, Buthelezi 'dedicated' a new administrative building for TEBA in the KwaZulu capital, Ulundi. Buthelezi welcomed the change that saw 60% of mining labour being recruited in South Africa in that year (as against 22% seven years earlier). He was especially 'glad to see Zulus return once again to mining'. He felt that both skills and 'the discipline of labour' were being transferred, and reminisced about a personal visit to a mine:

I have thought of it, that such work situations with their heavy demands on discipline and endurance are a far better training ground than any of the so-called guerilla camps outside the country, in making us men among men (quoted Maré and Hamilton, 1987:50).

The Chamber of Mines journal *Mining Survey*, where author Dennis Gordon had quoted Buthelezi's homilies on mine labour, offered a fascinating glimpse into the manner in which mine management perceived Zulu ethnicity. Gordon described Buthelezi as 'Chief Minister of the partially self-governing state of KwaZulu...also a Prince of the Zulu Royal Family, leader of the Inkatha movement...and one of Africa's most influential voices'. TEBA district manager, Bill Larkan, was said to have a 'deep commitment to the Zulu nation'; while other TEBA officials are described as believing 'that the traditional discipline to which rural Zulus are still subjected through the tribal structure of chiefs and headmen fits men for work on the Mines' (quoted Maré and Hamilton, 1987:50). In 1982 TEBA announced its sponsorship of a newspaper for 70 000 KwaZulu school children.

In 1987 the longest mining strike in South Africa's history, involving the largest number of workers (about 250 000), took place over wage demands. Thirty-three of the 99 coal and gold mines were involved and some 50 000 workers were dismissed. Two weeks before the strike was settled, on 13 August, Buthelezi addressed the 'TEBA 75th Anniversary Gala Dinner' (BS, 13.08.87). He praised TEBA for looking after miners and being 'a friend of my people because it is the recruiting agency which takes people from their homes to the mines where they can do that which their wisdom tells them they should do'. He also warned against 'Those in the labour movements who use trade unionism for political purposes.' This warning came a year after Inkatha had formed its Uwusa, which was subsequently funded by the security police.

The second mining example involves the king who, in 1986, had been brought into the fray to counter the organising success of the Cosatu-affiliated National Union of Mineworkers in the heartland of the new 'Zulu kingdom', Northern Natal and Zululand. The king had by now become an effective extension of the regional ethnic mobilisation, a far cry from the time when he was reprimanded by Buthelezi in 1973 for taking up workers' grievances. On this occasion, Goodwill addressed a gathering – which included mine managers, a South African cabinet minister, and chiefs and their councillors – to open the Zululand Anthracite Colliery. He claimed, as usual, to 'rise above politics' and then sharply criticised NUM and Cosatu officials for undermining the 'free enterprise system'. He then warned some miners who made 'a habit' of insulting Buthelezi that they should desist. King Goodwill appealed to the same social identity as Buthelezi did in his address to KwaZulu police in early 1987, when he reminded colliery workers that

> *We come from a warrior race and we know that true power*
> *gives gentleness to those who have it where gentleness is*
> *demanded... It is my hope that people who work in this colliery*
> *will conduct themselves with dignity... We do not discriminate*
> *against other Blacks who come to work here because KwaZulu*
> *is part of South Africa. They are our brothers. But they must*
> *behave themselves and respect Black leadership of this region*
> *(GS, 23.05.86).*

A few days after the king's speech, NUM members at Hlobane
Colliery were attacked by Uwusa members, supported by mine
management and allegedly by an outside group of Inkatha
supporters. At least 11 died during the violence and many were
injured.

The third example involves farmers and Inkatha. It was in the
agricultural district of Ngotshe that Inkatha most clearly brought in
its tradition of control through ethnicity. In August 1986 the
Ngotshe Co-operation Agreement was signed between some
farmers in the Ngotshe district in Northern Natal and Inkatha on
behalf of agricultural workers and African 'squatters' on
white-owned farms in the district. The agreement allowed Inkatha
unprecedented access to farm workers, notoriously inaccessible to
union organisers; it also reintroduced chiefs, who had been evicted
from white-owned land, to 'restore the disciplinary structures of
the Zulu hierarchy in our district', as Tjaart van Rensburg,
chairperson of the Ngotshe Co-operation Committee, told King
Goodwill Zwelethini (quoted Maré and Hamilton, 1987a).

The Ngotshe district had several problems to deal with in the
mid-1980s:

- it was situated on the border with Swaziland and was believed
  to be a transit route for ANC guerillas;
- a number of 'labour farms' existed in the district, owned by
  absentee landlords (Van Rensburg told the *Farmer's Weekly*
  (10.03.86) that these labour farms were 'units with no
  discipline' and that 'the intention of the agreement is to repair
  the disciplinary structure');
- chiefs had been evicted from the area;

- and white farmers felt threatened by Cosatu's moves to organise farm workers.

The agreement involved a range of objectives, including development, improving education, guaranteeing security for farm workers and labour-farm occupants, and *safeguarding the traditional Zulu way of life.*

In meetings prior to the agreement, Van Rensburg told the king that 'It is our sincere wish to restore the disciplinary structures of the Zulu hierarchy in our district'; later he said that 'Our aim is now to return the chiefs to their original place of residence with their families where they will once more form the nucleus of the area and maintain discipline'. The coincidence of interests between Inkatha and the farmers around discipline through 'tradition' was complete.

In Richmond, several years later the scene of months of violent clashes between Inkatha and ANC supporters, attempts were made to replicate the Ngotshe agreement in the late 1980s. Once more the participants were white farmers and Inkatha. The Richmond Regional Development Association argued that

> *we should discuss with the leaders in these tribal areas some form of accord which would prevent the influx of irresponsible trade union movements that would break down the present predominantly good relations which exist on most farms and to encourage the tribal authorities and farm labour to join the Inkatha Movement which is private enterprise orientated rather than the trade unions which are not (quoted Maré and Hamilton, 1987a).*

Inkatha, Uwusa and its leaders played an extremely conservative role in the mid-1980s, which included attempts to discipline and control the working class. This was clearly appreciated by people such as Jan van der Horst, chairperson of the giant Old Mutual group:

> *I recently saw Chief Buthelezi. We talked very openly. To my mind our future lies in that direction, because we are dealing*

with a Christian, we are dealing with a man who has Western habits, and who believes in certain Western things such as private enterprise, the business of ownership, and so on. Chief Buthelezi is the leader of a most important tribe (Leadership South Africa, 5(6), 1986).

Chapter Five

'The King and I'

During the first half of the 1970s, there were a number of state attempts to dislodge Buthelezi and form a more pliable leadership around the Zulu king. Security and information organs of the state, in particular, reasoned that Buthelezi did not serve the essential purpose of taking KwaZulu to 'independence', and that an alternative repository of 'tradition', the king, was available. In an attempt to capture ethnic symbols in their fight against another ethnic project, parties formed in opposition to Buthelezi and Inkatha used names like Inala (named after one of the king's regiments and also one of his residences) and Shaka's Spear.

Buthelezi, however, had already sidelined the king into a symbolic figurehead of the 'Zulu nation'. In 1972 the KwaZulu constitution was altered to reflect this supra-political position Buthelezi wanted for the king. He intended to control the monarch through the patronage of the KLA. In 1974, for example, Buthelezi told the KLA that King Goodwill, as the 'king of four-and-a-quarter million Zulus in South Africa', deserved the expenditure of R300 000 on a palace. 'If the Zulus want a monarchy they must pay for it', he argued. 'I mean, for instance, just across here the king of Swaziland has not one palace, but a number of them. And the Swazi nation, with all due respect to them, is a smaller nation than the Zulu nation...' (*KLAD*, 4, 1974:360).

By 1982 the king had no fewer than three palaces and many other trappings of his 'traditional' position, and had become part of

Inkatha's political project. Since then, the king's function has involved two central elements: to give symbolic coherence to the 'Zulu nation' and to issue orders in its name; and to confer legitimacy on Buthelezi as the central political representative of the same 'nation'.

Let me present an example of how this construction works. The event is one of the 'King Shaka Day' celebrations in 1991, held in this case in Eshowe in Zululand on 24 September. Buthelezi introduces the king to the assembled KwaZulu, consular, religious, royal and other dignitaries, and to the 'sons and daughters of Africa'. Before he presents a history of the achievements of Shaka and the kings after him, Buthelezi says that

> *Whenever I have to stand up to introduce His Majesty the King of the Zulu on these formal cultural occasions, I burn with a deep sense of pride. It is when one focuses on His Majesty representing the unity of the people in his person, and when you focus on His Majesty summing up Zulu history in his person, that you are confronted with an overwhelming sense of who the Zulu people actually are. What makes it so special is that most of the Zulu Kings are forbears to both of us (South African Update, 3(9), September 1991).*

The king then responds and says that each place he visits confirms for him 'who we are' – Eshowe 'itself really is the domain of the Zulu people', having been the site of King Mpande's palace, Cetshwayo's birthplace, Dingane's kraal, place of residence of Dinuzulu, and so on. The king confirms Buthelezi's call that the 'real power of the Zulus is in their unity, in their purpose and in their collective voice which says yea or nay and then yea or nay it will be'. He affirms that Zulus are a 'warrior nation', fashioned by history, but says that such 'warrior blood' strengthens 'not our arm only...(but also) our resolve to do good and our resolve to be gentle, and our resolve to spread power based on discussion and consensus'.

Goodwill functions primarily as a symbol, rather than a major actor:

> *I today want to thank my uncle, the Prince of KwaPhindangene*
> *Prince Mangosuthu Buthelezi, for what he is doing to bring*
> *about Black unity... My people, I know my uncle and he and I*
> *represent the indivisibility of the nation... Put first things first*
> *and trust the history that first created the great Zulu nation and*
> *then went on to create the great Zulu empire and then went*
> *further on to take that which it created and make it a force for*
> *the establishment of a new South Africa (GS, 25.09.89).*

He draws the boundaries of exclusion and inclusion of the Zulu
ethnic group very clearly – those who accept him accept Zuluness:
'History has put me where I am and all Zulu history demands that
I make the unity of my people my very first priority' (GS,
25.09.89).

And finally, Goodwill provides an alternative entity that can
live on after apartheid, into a regional future – the Zulu kingdom.
Many speeches in the late 1980s stress a Zulu contribution to
national change, with the emphasis on cultural and 'national'
diversity. King Goodwill told a 1990 Shaka Day gathering that 'I
am always very proud when I think of the extent to which the
Zulu nation has been there at every twist and turn of history to
play its role in shaping the new South Africa...' (GS, 23.09.90).

However, since the early 1980s, the king has not been allowed
to be a politically active leader with an effective and autonomous
power base. That role is only possible through his uncle and
'prime minister'. Buthelezi, like the king, claims the attributes that
are deemed to be part of being 'Zulu'. But unlike the king, he is
placed in an executive leadership role. So, for example, he told the
Inkatha Youth Brigade that 'I come from a very long line of
distinguished Zulu generals which goes right back to the great
King Shaka himself' (BS, 22.08.87). The unqualified nature of this
claim suggests that it is natural that he should lead as a general.
The king affirms this view when he frequently refers to Buthelezi
as a warrior or as located within the line of Zulu warriors.

This use of 'the past' has sometimes necessitated the blatant
alteration of research findings. In 1984, for example, a copy of the
revised draft of the text of the KwaZulu Monuments Council

publication *Fight Us in the Open* (Laband, 1985) was submitted for comment to Oscar Dhlomo, then KwaZulu minister of education and culture and Inkatha secretary general. Dhlomo raised two objections to the text, both of them involving 'Prime Minister (to Cetshwayo) Myamana Buthelezi', Mangosuthu Buthelezi's great-grandfather and an essential link in the prominent political role Buthelezi claims within the 'Zulu nation'.

The first objection involved Cetshwayo's narrative which 'gives the impression', wrote Dhlomo, 'that Prime Minister Mnyamana Buthelezi delivered the King (Cetshwayo, in 1879) to Sir Garnet Wolseley'. Dhlomo said that the impression 'is clearly unacceptable as it will cause a lot of conflict among the Zulus':

> *You will surely understand that many Zulu people who will read the manuscript will not appreciate the scientific fact that this is a mere record of the testimony of historical witnesses. They will take the testimony as gospel truth (Forsyth, 1989:appendix B).*

The editors obliged, and Laband's book (1985:37) does not contain those lines.

The second objection was to evidence that some warriors fighting the British in 1879 complained of poor generalship by Mnyamana. Laband qualified the evidence in the original text, indicating that its truth was not established. However, this was not enough and Dhlomo wrote that 'This allegation will also have serious implications'. It, too, was removed from the final version.

'Kingdom' and regional base

> *In the fortress-like mountains and forests of Nkandla, on the southern border of Zululand, (Bambatha) began to build up an army of resistance... In the Nkandla, Bambatha, joined by a number of prominent chiefs, conducted guerilla warfare against the white troops for nearly a month, making use of (Zulu king) Dinuzulu's name as his authority and using also the war-cry and war-badge of the Zulu kings (Marks, 1970:xv-xvi).*
> *'Wherever there is a Zulu, he or she must be made aware*

> *that the final expression of Zulu respect for my own leadership
> and my own line of descent must be expressed in Zulu national
> pride in the way people vote in elections and referendums,' he
> (Buthelezi) said.*
>
> *'If we fail in making the people aware of what has taken
> place in the past and what is happening now, the ANC will
> finally succeed in smashing Zulu pride in who we are and where
> we come from.'*
>
> *Whatever else happened, regionalism would be entrenched as
> important in the new South Africa, Dr Buthelezi maintained
> (Daily News, 24.03.92).*

The politicised ethnicity of Buthelezi and his followers could
result in a number of scenarios. The least problematic of these
involves the regionalisation of a future South Africa. All parties at
the Convention for a Democratic South Africa (Codesa) subscribe
to some form of regionalism, even though the IFP and the NP are
its strongest advocates. A federal system will serve as the vehicle
through which Buthelezi will attempt to create the 'Indaba Natal'
envisaged and so vigorously pursued in 1986 and 1987. If open
political competition – marked by the right and the ability to hold
meetings, disseminate ideas, organise and differ – accompanies
such a federal decentralisation, it will allow both nationally--
directed politics and various strands of 'Zuluness' and other ethnic
identities within a common arena to dilute the exclusive claims of
Inkatha. Twenty per cent of the regional population (whites and
Indians) is immediately excluded from potential membership of
the Zulu ethnic identity before a single shot has been fired over
claims to the allegiance of those who live in Natal.

However, there is the potential for another version of federal
decentralisation in Natal. This takes into consideration Buthelezi's
extreme claims of exclusive representation within the 'Zulu
nation', and the history of anti-democratic practice across the
political spectrum. In this Natal, only destabilisation will allow
Buthelezi effective (if undemocratic) control. The structures set up
under apartheid in KwaZulu will continue to hold sway, including
chiefship and the regional police force.

Confronted from 1990 with an unbanned ANC, ethnic mobilisation within the Inkatha strategy has, if anything, increased. Buthelezi and other Inkatha leaders have linked even discredited or controversial institutions such as bantustans (KwaZulu in this case), migrant labour single-sex hostels, and chiefs' authority, to the 'Zulu nation'. As the king said in 1990:

> Sadly, tragically even, there are some in South Africa who just
> do not understand the depth of commitment of Zulu to Zulu.
> They do not understand that when you insult one Zulu, you
> insult every Zulu. They do not understand that when you insult
> KwaZulu as such, every Zulu is insulted ad every Zulu worthy
> of the name will stand up and say enough is enough (GS,
> 23.09.90).

When the ANC and Cosatu called for the dismantling of KwaZulu as a political structure and the scrapping of the KwaZulu police force, Buthelezi claimed this was an attack on the 'Zulu nation' and on the king. He claimed that all Zulus were affronted:

> I hope that the Zulu people whatever their political affiliations
> will realise that the ANC campaign of vilification is no longer
> just against me and Inkatha but also against the Zulu people as
> Zulu people... KwaZulu is not a construct of apartheid and this
> is known even by a primary school child who knows the outline
> of Zulu history (BS, 09.08.90).

Inkatha was, in part, formed to secure a regional base as a platform to launch into national politics. It aimed to secure that base through political structures and agents, and through the ideology of the 'Zulu nation'. However, the costs of working within the system, and the extremes of co-operation with the apartheid state in defending privileges inextricably tied to the bantustan and politicised ethnicity, were waiting to be exposed. That moment arrived when the extent of Inkatha's involvement in the state's 'counter-insurgency' strategy was revealed. This involvement went beyond the 'normal' integration demanded of participants in apartheid. Inkatha had chosen to co-operate with the most vicious agents of the 'total strategy' set in place by PW Botha.

It is ironic that the 200 Inkatha members selected to be trained by the SADF in Northern Namibia should have been there when journalist Michael Massing was in South Africa, interviewing Buthelezi. Massing described Buthelezi's anti-communism, 'tribal appeals to solidify his ethnic and regional bases', his travels to and warm relationship with free enterprise-supporting Western Europe, USA and Israel, and the way in which Inkatha members were being armed. And, importantly, Massing 'was struck by its growing similarities to Unita' (Massing, 1987).

Although Inkatha's strategy of regional consolidation was originally intended as a basis for national politics, this has now changed. The unbanning of the ANC, and the exposés of Inkatha involvement with military intelligence and the security police, has probably convinced Buthelezi and his advisers that regional consolidation, and with it extreme ethnic consolidation, must become ends in themselves. The new mobilisation of the 'Zulu nation' has, to some extent, cut the tie with Inkatha. Inkatha recently became the Inkatha Freedom Party, open to all 'races'. It could not claim to be the party of the 'Zulu nation' without alienating non-Zulus. In addition, a wider mobilisation in the region necessitated that the king be brought to centre stage. For there were indications that Inkatha represented a small minority of Zulu-speakers, even in Natal.

Why is a 'Zulu renaissance', beyond Inkatha but within KwaZulu, necessary for this project of regional consolidation? There are several reasons: it is a mobilising ideology that does not threaten the class interests and aspirations of the petty bourgeois leadership of Inkatha; it gives greater legitimacy to the strategy of working through tribal structures, so necessary for control and organisation; it bolsters the chiefs ideologically in a situation where they have no basis of authority other than naked repression or corrupt manipulation of favours; it allows Buthelezi and the king to offer a supposedly disciplined 'constituency' to whatever backers they still have in current power plays; it is an essential aspect of the personal legitimation of Buthelezi and of the king; and it creates the possibility of power and influence in any future federal structure of government in South Africa.

These all aim to advance the organised form of Zulu ethnicity, and more recently a 'Zulu nation', to be consolidated through the king, under Buthelezi, and through the KwaZulu bantustan.

The mobilisers of ethnicity during the 1970s and 1980s did not merely 'switch on' or 'create' a Zulu ethnic identity. That identity was there, located in a regional history of conquest and colonialism. But it did not exist as a politically mobilised and organisationally exclusive group, nor did it have a defined set of symbols and attributes. This could occur only as a result of apartheid and the social disruption it caused, whereby the creation of ethnic politics and ethnic enclaves allowed free rein to those willing to participate. In KwaZulu, as in all the bantustans, traders and a new petty bourgeoisie in the top echelons of the civil service benefited most from the 'ethnic curtains' which protected them from competition.

Inkatha's dominant 'tradition' involves Zulu ethnicity (an ethnic populism) which depends in content, structures and agents on the apartheid system. And the regional political direction which Inkatha leaders have committed the movement to depends on the same consolidation of an ethnic and regional base.

The ethnic exclusivism of Buthelezi and other Inkatha leaders has led to a racially exclusive position. They argue that it is not possible for people of other 'races' to understand either the culture or plight of Zulus and Africans generally. An Inkatha leader involved in the conflict in Pietermaritzburg attacked the UDF in the following terms: 'The worst is that the UDF has a diverse membership, whereas Inkatha has only black people (ie Africans) as its members. The UDF just doesn't care what is happening in the townships', said Ben Jele (*Natal Witness*, 17.11.87). The same sentiments had been expressed about the ANC in the KwaZulu Legislative Assembly, many years before.

The 'traditions' used by Inkatha have served to both mobilise and control people. They mobilised the Inkatha movement as the organisational representation of Zulu and national liberation; they mobilised structures of control; they mobilised against opposition from within and from without, consolidating against class opponents, and crushing internal dissent; they mobilised people into a 'constituency', now being offered as a bargaining pawn in the national power play at Codesa; they mobilised to advance class interests, reflected in the aggressive pro-capitalist stance of Inkatha.

The presence of the past in the Natal region owes much to a specific set of symbols and history of resistance, but it is also indebted to the manner in which apartheid policy froze and distorted the past. This enabled the modern manipulators of an ethnic and regional past to emphasise the divisive aspects of politicised ethnicity. In their 'attempt to establish continuity with a suitable historical past' and provide social cohesion through 'conventions of behaviour', Inkatha leaders are burdened with what the apartheid state has made of history. The state's social cement is politicised ethnicity. This is also the case for Buthelezi and those around him.

Within the media, from social commentators to academics, and in the common-sense of public thinking, the idea of ethnicity as a basic political identity lives on. In the December 1987 judgment in the case of *Mangosuthu Gatsha Buthelezi vs Denis Becket and Saga Press (642/87)*, for example, where Buthelezi successfully sued *Frontline* magazine for defamation, Justice Howard found that

> *some allowance must surely be made for the fact that much of his (Buthelezi's) rhetoric (the 'bellicose passages' threatening violence to people who, for example, muddied his name) is designed to appeal to the instincts of the warrior nation he leads, the overriding object being the politically important one of preserving his constituency .*

The way in which a political version of the 'Zulu nation' has been created supports the argument that ethnicity should not be politically privileged. For it is in freezing a changing, 'created' and contested identity that conflict lies.

Section Three

Conclusion

Chapter Six

The Failure of Politicised Ethnicity

There is nothing mystical and holy about ethnic identities – they demand analysis, exposure and demystification. Guy and Thabane (1987) wrote that:

> *(T)he existence of ethnic prejudice, rivalry and violence amongst Africans is one fact of Southern African life – and to analyse it in the hope of explaining it, is a prerequisite to gaining greater control over it.*

This discussion has suggested some ways in which to conceptualise ethnicity – a social identity that shapes people's behaviour through the way they interpret the world. Ethnicity can meet real needs of security, or it can tip insecurity into exclusivist mobilisation and fuel antagonistic organisations and violence. It can express cultural variety within a larger commonality, or it can serve to demarcate insular social groupings fearful of their existence. However, ethnicity is but one of several powerful social identities that fulfil such roles.

Ethnic social identities and ethnic group consciousness have now been tied inextricably to violence in South Africa. The racism of colonial conquest and slavery and the years of segregation in the Union of South Africa; the sacred history of the Afrikaner volk with its claims to a God-given mission in Africa; and the vicious consequences of the implementation of apartheid, a policy based on separation – all these repressively enforced 'group politics' have involved violence. Little chance has been offered to de-emphasise group consciousness in the political field. Such a de-emphasis need not entail the denial of cultural variety, ethnic consciousness, or the desirability of a range of social identities. It should, however, shift these into a democratic practice within *society* (an encompassing social structure, capable of acknowledging and welcoming variety) as a whole.

Such an approach will demand enormous change, not simply a glib commitment to a single 'nation', or 'a united democratic South Africa'. The *problem* of ethnicity, which involves the manner in which it has been mobilised for conflictual politics, is not going to be solved through a centralised parliament making legislation. Neither will it be solved through denial of the phenomenon, or once. apartheid has been abolished.

Ethnicity as a social identity needs to be separated from political mobilisation, manipulation and fanning of ethnic sentiments. Ethnic groups should, therefore, not be constitutionally rewarded for their group identity. In much the same way, no other *social* identity should be so rewarded. The ethnic identities held by individuals should be protected in a bill of rights based on individual rights and freedoms. Religious groups, language groups, and so on, should not be rewarded with a special *group* dispensation, other than the rights of individuals to practice and to be protected in these areas. Why, therefore, should an equivalent identity – ethnicity – claim such reward? Only because, for some politicians, ethnicity is an available mobilising strategy of considerable strength which tends to hide class and gender divisions that might otherwise derail the projects of such cultural brokers and entrepreneurs.

However, politicised ethnicity is a reality in South Africa, as it is in many parts of the world. To resolve conflict where ethnicity motivates immediate behaviour, it will have to be 'sensitively and self-consciously depoliticised and severed from the arena of competition for resources, privilege, power and rights in future transformation' (Maré, 1987).

The Indaba constitution, with its powerful second house and its

racialised and ethnic representation, is still the model referred to
by both the National Party and Inkatha Freedom Party. The NP is
having enormous difficulty in shaking off its past emphasis on
'groups', while for the IFP, 'group' and regional solutions will
allow it an influence despite its absence of national strength.
Ironically, the NP has been forced to distance itself from some of
the excesses of ethnic division, because it has the potential of
wider mobilisation, especially amongst coloured people. Inkatha,
on the other hand, exists essentially as an ethnic party (albeit on
national platforms) through a regionalised ethnic appendage (the
'Zulu kingdom').

Politicised ethnicity arises, in large part, out of frustrated
economic and political goals. The next step in depoliticising
ethnicity therefore involves alteration of those economic relations
which currently give ethnic mobilisation its politicising spark. The
factors that make a population available for ethnic identity
formation need to be separated from the sparks that politicise and
give a conflictual edge to ethnicity.

Ethnicity must not be rewarded politically. But, at the same
time, the range of alternative group identities and organisations
need to be strengthened with the self-conscious purpose of
removing ethnicity as the only 'obvious' presence at this level of
social representation. This should involve women's organisations,
trade unions, churches, sports bodies, and local-level democratic
structures involved in housing, services and education. Political
parties or the 'national liberation movement', on the other hand,
are not particularly good vehicles for the strengthening of group
identities in opposition to ethnicity. They operate too directly in
the field where politicised ethnicity competes for space, rewards
and members. It is too easy, in the absence of a coherent policy on
cultural diversity, to conflate political organisations either with an
alternative ethnic identity ('the ANC is Xhosa') or with an
antagonism to 'Zulu' or other identities.

Patrick Wright, in exploring British conservative glorification
of 'living in the old country', wrote:

If we are to consider this Conservative [notion of the British] nation carefully, it must surely be with a view to discovering other possible articulations of cultural particularity, articulations which are respectful of the heterogeneity of contemporary society and also capable of making a coherent political principle of difference... (1985:26).

Let there indeed be a greater expression of cultural particularity in this society, but let it be articulated according to democratic principles and let it therefore also reflect a truly heterogeneous society rather than the unitary image of a privileged national identity which has been raised to the level of exclusive and normative essence (1985:255).

Wright has captured two desirable movements within society: the first acknowledges and makes 'a coherent political principle of difference', while the second argues against a 'privileged national identity' which does not allow variety.

Both of these demand the removal of ethnic identities from political reward and competition. On the other hand, they also demand that ethnicity be taken seriously. This is especially important where cultural resources are at stake (language and education, for example), and where regional allocation of material welfare is decided.

Journalist Carmel Rickard has warned against the 'ANC's insistence on unity' that 'might be weakening it as a unifying force'. She referred to Dr DF Malan's call to an Afrikaner ethnic identity in the election of 1948 that placed the National Party in power and launched this country into the misery of apartheid for the next 40 years, and commented that 'Malan's victory shows the danger of not having a policy which takes into account those people who rally to the call of the volk' (*Weekly Mail*, 30.05.91). One cannot simply deny the importance of politicised ethnicity as a potent mobilising factor because it runs counter to national plans for unity. Sensitivity has to be shown towards those elements of cultural diversity and the celebration of the past, at the same time ensuring that they are not manipulated into political mobilisation. Ethnicity should neither be privileged, nor should it be granted a special status through prosecution or denial.

Institutions are necessary to open debate on diversity, and provide the space to engage in both general cultural and more specific ethnic confirmation. The central imposition of a forced national identity is likely to fuel those conservative interests likely to support the 'Savimbi option' during any transitional phase. Rather, it is important to demonstrate that ethnic diversity can, at appropriate (ie non-politically prescribed) levels, be accommodated – in language policy, educational systems, cultural recognition (museums, festivals, the media), and so forth.

The notions of non-racialism, democracy and non-sexism are idealist, and have to be created out of their opposites, out of a history that had confirmed racism, a profoundly anti-democratic polity and patriarchy. On the other hand, ethnic identities and ethnic group formation arise out of a real sense of a unique past, a clearly distinct culture, and the actual existence of the ethnic group, even if only as imagined community. The denial of what exists in favour of the ideal, especially when ethnic leadership presents that ideal in terms of ethnic competition, carries the seeds of massive conflict.

The 'national liberation movement' and the ANC have most often been burdened with the task of building an over-arching social identity in South Africa. This is likely, in the near future, to fall to an ANC-controlled state. However, this is not where the solution to politicised ethnicity and national identity lies. Rather, the most important tasks lie in developing *civil society*, that vast area of structures and interactions between people that are not immediately related to centralised authority and power. Unfortunately, the centralisation of repression through the racial, class and gender exclusivity of the apartheid state has frequently shaped opposition into a mirror image of that state. This has allowed little space for dissent and independence in 'the struggle'.

Nation-building will be a most difficult task in the South African context. While a commitment to democracy (and there are plenty of constitutional, rhetorical and sloganeering undertakings and commitments to a democratic future) of necessity includes respect for variety and the 'heterogeneity' of society, the daily reality of life is a marked and violent absence of such respect.

Political dissent has frequently been seen as the automatic justification for death.

Moving beyond politicised ethnicity lies in strengthening the horizontal rather than the vertical interests in society. This involves emphasising the issues and identities of class and gender, rather than ethnicity. These issues have a reality, even if they cannot compete with ethnicity as a package: class identity does not ring with the same clarity as 'the past' in ethnic mobilisation, does not exist primarily on the symbolic level of cultural signs, and creates a group only through the connection of labour.

Responding to the use of history to shape and motivate ethnic group identity is equally difficult. Great sensitivity will have to be shown in developing a nationally-propagated history, disseminated through the media, through education, through the practice of statecraft.

Far from being somehow 'behind' the present, the past exists as an accomplished presence in public understanding. In this sense it is written into present social reality, not just implicitly as residue, precedent or custom and practice, but explicitly as itself – as History, National Heritage and Tradition (Wright, 1985:142).

Wright suggests that there are pointers as to how this difficult task might be undertaken. For example, 'the "past" has been substantially rearranged so that it now contains a wider acknowledgement of, for instance, women and the working class' (1985:142). Through such expansion of the past other groups (social identities) can be given an identity that is wider than ethnic particularity, or ethnicity can be made more complex by looking at the class and gender divisions within that identity. Criticism of the 'past' should, however, not be detrimental to 'everyday historical consciousness – of stories, memory and vernacular interpretations...' (Wright, 1985:143), which form an essential part of social life.

Furthermore, it is not possible to offer a simple alternative to a 'wrong' history presented in an ethnic 'past'. Wright has warned

111

against such treatment of 'national (or ethnic) traditions and institutions as if they were merely contested items in a claim over inheritance. They have no such singularity and come with whole philosophies of history attached' (1985:155).

Ethnic groups are based on a complex interaction of the past, of cultural uniqueness, and of group boundaries. Tackling one aspect of this interaction severs only one head of the dragon and, to continue the metaphor, ignores the environment in which the dragon has thrived.

Jamba at Nkandla?

The politicisation of Zulu ethnicity during the 1970s and 1980s occurred within the political boundaries created by apartheid. Consequently, the political practice of Inkatha's leadership is to be found not only in the ethnic group that has been created, not only in the organisational form that it has been given through Inkatha, but also in the structures that have been created within the bantustan to administer 'Zulus' – that is, the KwaZulu government.

Buthelezi warned of the serious consequences if the KwaZulu government (equated with a 'Zulu kingdom' and the 'Zulu nation') was ignored. These warnings have now come to include even the structures of regional and ethnic class advancement. For example, in rejecting a proposed National Rural Development Corporation, Buthelezi defended the KwaZulu Finance and Investment Corporation (KFC) and asked that this body be 'mandated to expand its role throughout this region' (*Daily News*, 04.06.91). He has made similar calls for the continuation of the KwaZulu Bureau for Natural Resources.

Once a central figure in Inkatha's regional consolidation strategy, and now director of research at the Human Sciences Research Council, Lawrence Schlemmer has noted that 'the IFP controls the regional administration of KwaZulu and could, theoretically, destabilise that administration if it were to fall into different political hands or have its powers or policies altered from above' (*Sunday Tribune*, 23.06.91). This undemocratic control over one of the structures of apartheid has allowed Inkatha access to national negotiations. It could also allow Inkatha to reject or ignore any regional or national majority vote against it. This raises the spectre of a Jamba, the bush headquarters of Unita in Angola, at Nkandla, the Zululand forest headquarters for Bambatha in his last stand against centralised white power at the turn of the century.

Moves to revive the Indaba proposals and enable regional political groupings to dictate the future form of a national political entity have recently emerged. The bantustan leaders of Bophuthatswana, the Ciskei and KwaZulu agreed in a document presented to President De Klerk that

> *the new regional or 'state' boundaries within South Africa should be formalised and constituted before the setting up of an interim government or Parliament. To this end, the three leaders concur, it might be necessary to conclude processes of negotiation within these 'states', which would then come together to negotiate a federal arrangement – not the other way around (Shaun Johnson, writing in Daily News, 08.05.92).*

Disentangling legitimate diversity from the structurally embedded politicised ethnicity of Inkatha, written on the region for 17 years already, will be a delicate and slow process. It will, sadly, continue to bring bloodshed to this region and the rest of South Africa. The formation of the IFP has opened up three directions of operation for Buthelezi and his supporters. The first is to function as a political party within a national negotiation context and into a post-apartheid era, where its strength lies largely in its alliance with other essentially ethnically-based parties (the NP, and other bantustans and parties that owe their existence to the tri-cameral parliament). The second is to continue with 'Zulu' mobilisation in its regional base, using 'tradition' and the symbolic figure of the king. The third involves the continuation of the bantustan (and increasingly regional, Natal-wide) structures of administration into the future (see Forsyth and Maré, 1992).

All three options are being followed at the same time. They all indicate that Buthelezi and his politics of politicised ethnicity have failed hopelessly as a force for bringing South Africans together.

References

Anderson, Benedict (1983): *Imagined Communities: reflections on the origin and spread of nationalism* (London: Verso)

Beall, Jo, Jeremy Grest, Heather Hughes and Gerhard Maré (1986): 'Conceptualising Natal: implications of a regional political economy' (paper for the seventeenth annual congress of the Association for Sociology in Southern Africa, University of Natal, Durban)

Berger, John (1991): *Once In Europa* (London: Granta Books)

Boonzaier, Emile and John Sharp (eds) (1988): *South African Keywords: the uses and abuses of political concepts* (Cape Town: David Philip)

Brink, Elsabe (1990): 'Man-made women: gender, class and the ideology of the *volksmoeder*', in Cherryl Walker (ed): *Women and Gender in Southern Africa to 1945* (Cape Town: David Philip)

BS (Buthelezi Speech, mimeo) (21.01.87): 'KwaZulu Police – Passing Out Parade. Speech by Mangosuthu G Buthelezi, Chief Minister and Minister of Police, KwaZulu. President of Inkatha and Chairman, The South African Black Alliance' (Emandleni)

BS (06.04.87): 'Unveiling of the tombstone of the late H Selby Msimang (Unkonkana WeFusi) founder-member of the banned African National Congress, and later Central Committee member of Inkatha, and of Mrs Mirriam Noluthando Msimang: tribute by Mangosuthu G Buthelezi...' (Georgetown Cemetery, Edendale)

BS (13.08.87): 'TEBA 75th Anniversary Gala Dinner' (Ulundi)

BS (22.08.87): 'The importance of conserving lives and energy and of preserving our manpower in preparing ourselves for the final battle in the struggle for liberation' (speech to Inkatha Youth Brigade Annual General Conference, Ulundi)

BS (24.09.88): 'King Shaka Day: address and presentation of His

Majesty to the people' (Stanger)

BS (23.03.90): 'Memorandum for discussion at a meeting with the Amakhosi and Mangosuthu Buthelezi...' (Ulundi)

BS (09.08.90): 'ANC's contempt for the Zulus and their King: press release' (Ulundi)

BS (13.09.90): 'Meeting with the Amakhosi of KwaZulu' (Ulundi)

BS (12.06.91): 'Memorandum by Mangosuthu Buthelezi...for a Discussion...with Senator Gareth Evans, Australian Foreign Minister, et al' (Ulundi)

BS (21.09.91): 'King Shaka Day: presentation of His Majesty the King of the Zulus to the people' (Stanger)

BS (18.01.92): 'Official Opening of Visitor Centre and Isandlwana Historic Reserve: introduction of His Majesty King Zwelethini Goodwill ka Bhekuzulu King of the Zulus' (Isandlwana)

Butler, Jeffrey (1989): 'Afrikaner women and the creation of ethnicity in a small South African town, 1902-1950', in Leroy Vail (ed): *The Creation of Tribalism in Southern Africa* (London: James Currey)

Chidester, David (1992): *Religions of South Africa* (London: Routledge)

Connor, Walker (1984): *The National Question in Marxist-Leninist Theory and Strategy* (Princeton, New Jersey: Princeton University Press)

Cope, NLG (1986): 'The Zulu royal family under the South African government 1910-1930: Solomon kaDinuzulu, Inkatha and Zulu nationalism' (unpublished PhD thesis, University of Natal, Durban)

Cronjé, G (1945): 'Die huisgesin in die Afrikaanse kultuurgemeenskap', in CM van den Heever and P de V Pienaar (eds): *Kultuurgeskiedenis van die Afrikaner*, vol 1 (Cape Town: Nasionale Pers)

DSG/SARS (Development Studies Group/Southern African Research Service) (1982): *The Land Dispute: incorporating Swaziland* (Johannesburg, Information Publication 7)

Fanon, Frantz (1970): *Black Skin White Masks* (London: Paladin)

February, Vernon (1991): *The Afrikaners of South Africa* (London: Kegan Paul)

Ferraro, Thomas J (1989): 'Blood in the marketplace: the business of family in the *Godfather* narratives', in Werner Sollors (ed): *The Invention of Ethnicity* (Oxford: Oxford University Press)

Forsyth, Paul (1989): 'The past as present: chief MG Buthelezi's use of history as a source of political legitimation' (unpublished MA dissertation, University of Natal, Pietermaritzburg)

Forsyth, Paul and Gerhard Maré (1992): 'Natal in the new South Africa', in Glenn Moss and Ingrid Obery (eds): *From 'Rooivrydag' to Codesa. South African Review 6* (Johannesburg: Ravan)

Giddens, Anthony (1989): *Sociology* (Cambridge: Polity Press)

GS (King Goodwill Zwelethini Speech) (23.05.86): 'Official opening of the Zululand Anthracite Colliery. Speech by His Majesty King Goodwill Zwelethini ka Bhekuzulu King of the Zulus' (Okhukho)

GS (16.06.86): 'Address to the Zulu Nation by His Majesty King Goodwill Zwelethini ka Bhekuzulu, King of the Zulus' (Mona Saleyards, Nongoma)

GS (24.09.86): 'King Shaka Day: Address by His Majesty King Goodwill Zwelethini ka Bhekuzulu, King of the Zulus' (King Shaka's Monument, Stanger)

GS (25.09.89): 'King Shaka Day' (Stanger)

GS (23.09.90): 'Celebration of King Shaka Day: address by His Majesty King Goodwill Zwelethini Ka Bhekezulu, King of the Zulus' (King's Park Stadium, Durban)

GS (26.05.91): 'Address to the Zulu Nation and to all South Africans' (First National Bank Stadium, Johannesburg)

Guy, Jeff (1990): 'Gender oppression in southern Africa's precapitalist societies', in Cherryl Walker (ed): *Women and Gender in Southern Africa to 1945* (Cape Town: David Philip)

Guy, Jeff and Mutlatsi Thabane (1987): 'Technology, ethnicity and ideology: Basotho miners and shaft sinking on the South African gold mines' (paper presented at Conference on *Culture et Politique en Afrique Australe*, Paris)

Hassim, Shireen (1992): 'Family, motherhood and Zulu nationalism: the politics of the Inkatha Women's Brigade'

(mimeo, forthcoming in *Feminist Review*, October)

Heller, Monica (1987): 'The role of language in the formation of ethnicity', in Jean S Phinney and Mary Jane Rotheram (eds): *Children's Ethnic Socialization: pluralism and development* (Newbury Park, Calif: Sage)

Hobsbawm, Eric and Terence Ranger (eds) (1984): *The Invention of Tradition* (Cambridge: Cambridge University Press)

Hogg, Michael A and Dominic Abrams (1988): *Social Identifications: a social psychology of intergroup relations and group processes* (London: Routledge)

IBS (Irene Buthelezi Speech) (20.05.90): 'Rally, Mothers, Rally – Rise up for History' (Mother's Day Celebrations, Ulundi)

Inkatha (1983): 'Inkatha: its viewpoints on change and liberation in South Africa' (mimeo, lodged Natal Room, University of Natal, Durban)

Inkatha Syllabus Committee (1978): 'The National Cultural Liberation Movement: syllabus for primary and secondary/high schools' (KwaZulu Government Service, Department of Education and Culture, mimeo)

Kentridge, Matthew (1990): *An Unofficial War: inside the conflict in Pietermaritzburg* (Cape Town: David Philip)

Khoapa, BA (ed) (1973): *Black Review 1972* (Durban: Black Community Programmes)

KLAD (KwaZulu Legislative Assembly Debates) (various years)

Laband, John (1985): *Fight Us in the Open* (Pietermaritzburg: Shuter and Shooter)

Le Roux, Pieter (1986): 'Growing up an Afrikaner', in Sandra Burman and Pamela Reynolds (eds): *Growing Up in a Divided Society* (Johannesburg: Ravan)

Lodge, Tom (1983): *Black Politics in South Africa since 1945* (Johannesburg: Ravan)

Louw-Potgieter, Joha (1988): *Afrikaner Dissidents: a social psychological study of identity and dissent* (Clevedon, Philadelphia: Multilingual Matters)

LRC (Legal Resources Centre and Human Rights Commission) (1991): 'The role of the KwaZulu Police. Impartial law enforcement or obstacle to peace?' (Durban, mimeo)

Mann, Michael (ed) (1983): *Student Encyclopedia of Sociology* (London: Macmillan)

Maré, Gerhard (1987): 'Last chance, limited option, or no go?', in Roberts, Karin and Graham Howe (eds): *New Frontiers: the KwaZulu/Natal debates* (Durban: IPSA, University of Natal)

Maré, Gerhard (1988/89): '"Education in a liberated zone": Inkatha and education in KwaZulu', in *Critical Arts*, 4(4/5)

Maré, Gerhard (1989): 'Inkatha and regional control: policing liberation politics', in *Review of African Political Economy*, 45/46

Maré, Gerhard and Georgina Hamilton (1987): *An Appetite for Power: Buthelezi's Inkatha and South Africa* (Johannesburg: Ravan; Bloomington and Indianapolis: Indiana University Press)

Maré, Gerhard and Georgina Hamilton (1987a): '"Human relations and not labour relations": restructuring in agriculture and the Ngotshe Cooperation Agreement', in *Africa Perspective*, new series 1(5/6)

Marks, Shula (1970): *Reluctant Rebellion: the 1906-1908 disturbances in Natal* (London: Oxford University Press)

Marks, Shula (1986): *The Ambiguities of Dependence in South Africa: class, nationalism, and the state in twentieth-century Natal* (Johannesburg: Ravan).

Massing, Michael (1987): 'The Chief', in *The New York Review of Books* (12 February)

McLellan, David (ed) (1977): *Karl Marx: selected writings* (Oxford: Oxford University Press)

Mdluli, Praisley (Blade Nzimande) (1987): 'Ubuntu-Botho: Inkatha's "People's Education"', in *Transformation*, 5

Meer, Fatima (1969): *Portrait of Indian South Africans* (Durban: Avon House)

Miles, Robert (1989): *Racism* (London: Routledge)

Moodie, T Dunbar (1980): *The Rise of Afrikanerdom: power, apartheid and Afrikaner civil religion* (Berkeley: University of California Press)

Morris, Mike (1986): 'UWUSA, Inkatha and COSATU: lessons from May Day', in *Work in Progress*, 43

119

Mzala (1988): *Gatsha Buthelezi: chief with a double agenda* (London: Zed)

O'Meara, Dan (1983): *Volkskapitalisme: class, capital and ideology in the development of Afrikaner Nationalism, 1934-1948* (Johannesburg: Ravan)

Peires, Jeff (1987): 'Ethnicity and pseudo-ethnicity in the Ciskei' (paper presented at conference on *Culture et Politique en Afrique Australe*, Paris)

Phizacklea, Annie and Robert Miles (1980): *Labour and Racism* (London: Routledge and Kegan Paul)

Ramsey, Patricia G (1987): 'Young children's thinking about ethnic differences', in Phinney and Rotheram (eds): *Children's Ethnic Socialization: pluralism and development* (Newbury Park, Calif: Sage)

Ranger, Terence (1989): 'Missionaries, migrants and the Manyika: the invention of ethnicity in Zimbabwe', in Leroy Vail (ed): *The Creation of Tribalism in Southern Africa* (London: James Currey)

Saul, John S (1979): 'The dialectic of tribe and class', in John S Saul: *The State and Revolution in Eastern Africa* (New York: Monthly Review Press)

Segal, Lauren (1991): 'The human face of violence: hostel dwellers speak' (seminar paper 6, Project for the Study of Violence, University of the Witwatersrand, Johannesburg)

Singh, Ratnamala and Shahid Vawda (1988): 'What's in a name?: some reflections on the Natal Indian Congress', in *Transformation*, 6

Sitas, Ari (1988): 'Class, nation, ethnicity in Natal's black working class' (paper presented at the *Workshop on Regionalism and Restructuring in Natal,* Local Government Project, University of Natal, Durban)

Smith, Anthony (1981): *The Ethnic Revival in the Modern World* (London: Cambridge University Press)

Sollors, Werner (1986): *Beyond Ethnicity: consent and descent in American culture* (New York: Oxford University Press)

Survey (South African Institute of Race Relations) (various years, as referenced in text): *Race Relations Survey* (Johannesburg:

SAIRR)

Suny, Ronald (1990): 'The revenge of the past: socialism and ethnic conflict in Transcaucasia', in *New Left Review*, 184

Swart, Richard (1984): (unpublished) 'Interview with Dr Oscar Dhlomo' (mimeo, Natal Room, University of Natal, Durban)

Temkin, Ben (1976): *Gatsha Buthelezi: Zulu Statesman* (Cape Town: Purnell)

Therborn, Göran (1980): *The Ideology of Power and the Power of Ideology* (London: Verso)

Thornton, Robert (1988): 'Culture: a contemporary definition', in Boonzaier and Sharp (eds): *South African Keywords: the uses and abuses of political concepts* (Cape Town: David Philip)

Van der Westhuysen, HM (1950): 'Kultuurbewuswording van die Afrikaner', in CM van den Heever and P de V Pienaar (eds): *Kultuurgeskiedenis van die Afrikaner: the eerste beskrywing van die Boere-volkslewe in al sy vertakkinge* (Cape Town: Nasionale Boekhandel)

Walker, Cherryl (1990): 'Women and gender in southern Africa to 1945: an overview', in Cherryl Walker (ed): *Women and Gender in Southern Africa to 1945* (Cape Town: David Philip)

Webster, David (1991): '*Abafazi BaThonga Bafihlakala*: ethnicity and gender in a KwaZulu border community', in AD Spiegel and PA McAllister (eds): *Tradition and Transition in Southern Africa* (Johannesburg: Witwatersrand University Press)

Webster, Eddie (1987): 'A profile of unregistered union members in Durban', in Johann Maree (ed): *The Independent Trade Unions 1974-1984: ten years of the South African Labour Bulletin* (Johannesburg: Ravan)

Williams, Raymond (1976): *Keywords: a vocabulary of culture and society* (Glasgow: Fontana)

Wright, John and Aron Mazel (1988): 'Controlling the past in the museums of Natal and KwaZulu' (paper presented at *Workshop on Regionalism and Restructuring in Natal,* Local Government Project, University of Natal, Durban)

Wright, Patrick (1985): *On Living in an Old Country: the national past in contemporary Britain* (London: Verso)

Index